TALES OF A FILM PROP MAN

TALES OF A FILM PROP MAN

PETE BENSON

atmosphere press

Published by Atmosphere Press

Cover design by Dhiraj Navlakhe

Atmospherepress.com

CHAPTER I

THE BEGINNING

Deep in the heart of the Kent countryside, in a sprawling country estate, there is a party going on. This is no ordinary party. Not one that mere mortals could ever dream of being invited to, for the guest list includes legendary Film Stars such as Elizabeth Taylor, Rock Hudson, Tony Curtis, Kim Novak, Geraldine Chaplin, Edward Fox and many others. As they sip their Daiquiris and the canapes arrive on silver trays, we hear polite conversation.

We are on the film set of the 1980s version of 'The Mirror Crack'd', another instalment in the magic of movies.

Behind the camera stands the Director, Guy Hamilton, and the rest of the crew. Guy watches every movement, every expression, listens to every word spoken. His judgement is final, and if he is not happy then they go again.

Guy is a director of some renown, having directed some 20 films during his career, including 4 'Bond' movies. This is a safe pair of hands.

This is a meeting of some of the Elite of the film industry and portrays a world that, to most people, they could only dream about being part of. How many kids have gazed saucer eyed at the big screen and wished that could be their life? I know I did as a youngster, along with being a Rock Star or professional footballer.

What I haven't told you is that standing just off set, ready to top-up drinks, replenish food, refresh plates and glasses and reset whatever needs to be done for the next take for this scene, are the Standby Prop Men. Incredibly, my dreams had come true for one of those Prop Men was me, and I was now working in the film industry, on this film set, being called by my first name and accepted as part of the unit.

Everything about this film epitomised to me what making films was all about. Big Stars, lavish sets, great locations, lights, cameras, the lot, and this film gave me an opportunity to meet and work with some of the greats of film production that I might never meet again.

I was leading a life where working with film stars, travelling the world, staying in big hotels, eating great food and being paid well for doing it had become the norm. I was even being called by my first name as if we were old friends. Life did seem surreal.

I will tell you more about this film later, as you are probably wondering how this all came about in the first place. If I had followed the path my education was leading me down, I would never have become a Prop Man and never have written this book. Fate played a vital part in all of this.

Back in 1978, I had some serious decisions to make. I was unemployed. My then wife, Ann, was pregnant with our first child, and we had a large mortgage hanging around our necks. Living in a sleepy village just along the coast from Folkestone in Kent, my job prospects didn't look good at all.

I had gone to university and obtained a Bachelor of Arts degree in Business finance. Ann was a qualified hairdresser, and we had moved to Folkestone and opened our own salon after I left my job in an office of a company making safes, and

Ann quit her job in a salon in St Albans in Hertfordshire. We both hated what we were doing and were looking for something else. The Salon didn't work out as we had planned, so I was doing whatever it took for us to get by, and my present job wasn't right either.

As I ambled along the beach at Sandgate just outside Folkestone, across from my previous employer, a well-known holiday firm, there was a cold wind blowing in off the sea. I had to smile, for I had just handed my notice in to a Mr. Frost. 'Freddie to everyone'.

The company was positively 'Orwellian' in its concept. Each day, around 500 workers would trudge up the long winding driveway to a converted mansion and manually process holiday forms and answer frantic calls from stranded pensioners all over the world. If we had been sitting at tall desks with quill pens, it would not have been out of place. Time had stood still in this building, and technology hadn't even knocked on the door.

How I had remained in their employment I do not know. They had promised me the earth on more than one occasion if I stayed, but this time I had called their bluff, and they had proven to have more reverse gears than an Italian tank. Today, they are a household name, and I often wonder what would have happened if I had just put my head down and stayed there.

Could I really have made a fulfilling career in a job I hated? Having experienced an alternative, I think the answer would have been a resounding "No".

I had made that decision now, and as I drove back to our house in Hythe, I wondered how I would explain to Ann what I had just done, for this was not the first time I had done this. I couldn't seem to find a job that I liked enough to stay and make a go of.

As I came through the front door, Ann shouted down to me from upstairs that my brother, Les, had called to say he was coming to see us at Easter. This was unusual, as he worked all the time, and so didn't often get the chance to get down to Hythe. This was to be the turning point in my life, although I didn't know it at the time.

I don't think Ann was particularly surprised when I told her I had left my job, as we had both been moaning about it for some time now, so I got off the hook quite lightly.

It was nice to see Les again. It had been a while since he last came down, and we had a lot to catch up on. I explained that the Folkestone jobs market wasn't exactly throwing opportunities my way, and I was at a loss to know where to go next. I was in mid-sentence when he just said it.

"Why don't you be a Prop Man?"

I was a little lost for words as I tried to process this bombshell. I had no aversion to hard work, but generally my jobs were 9 to 5 and 5 days a week. Les's work had no bounds, and long hours with no time off were extremely common, with the money and sometimes exotic locations making up for the disadvantages.

Besides, I had a clapped-out Austin 1300 car, and the nearest studio to me was a hundred miles away. If I made it there, I'm not sure I would get back home in this vehicle. I said I'd talk it over with Ann and let him know, as getting into this industry would cause a huge change to our way of living and probably mean me being away from home a lot, a prospect I am not sure either of us was ready for. We discussed it long and hard, but something else Les had said kept coming into my mind.

"Why don't you try it for a couple of years, make a bit of money, until you decide what you want to do with your life?" he had said.

The fact was he was right, and I had no real alternative, so I phoned him and asked him if he could help me. I think he was quite pleased with that.

Back in the 1970s, becoming a Prop Man wasn't just a matter of turning up when asked. The Film Industry was heavily Unionised, and you needed someone to propose you and someone to second you, both of whom had to be working Prop Men themselves. Les proposed me, and a good friend of ours, John Palmer, seconded me, and then I had to go before The Prop Guild Committee, who were there to 'grill' me and find out if I was suitable or not.

Off I set in my old Austin, praying it would get me there, feeling extremely nervous. This was a big moment in my life, and I didn't want to waste it. As I stood there, I realised I hardly knew anyone, and *I* didn't know if I was suitable, let alone convince them, but they were all nice, and it seemed to go well. All sorts went through my mind on the way home, and fortunately, my 'trusted steed' got me back to Hythe. Now, I just had to wait.

Two weeks later, the letter arrived accepting me as a Prop Man. This was quite something as they were only taking on 6 new members that year and I was one of them.

I paid my membership fee and got my Union card, as without it I couldn't work, and the Union was very hot on this, making spot checks on Productions to make sure everything was in order. All I had to do now was get a job, but the journey up and down to the interview had pointed out a very deep flaw in my plans. My car was just not up to this sort of punishment and would need sorting.

Also, the roads currently were not so user-friendly, and from where I lived, the journeys would be on some dire roads that were always prone to hold ups. If I had to be somewhere and had to make up time, this Austin 1300 would not be the vehicle to do it in, so I had to invest money I could ill afford and give it a good service and check-over.

The news from the garage was not good. It shouldn't have been on the road, so I needed to scrap it and buy something else, which was even more money I didn't have.

Eventually, I ended up with a used green Ford Capri, which compared to the 1300 was like a Maserati. Although I was now more in debt, I did feel good driving it around.

My new career lay before me and ultimately led me to sitting here knocking out 40 to 60 thousand words on a keyboard. It reminds me of something Michelle Obama said recently when she was asked about Barack running for President. She said that he had asked her if she would support him if he ran and, after some thought, agreed. Later she wondered if she had said no and Barack had not run, then history could have been so different in so many ways.

Those little decisions at the time that don't appear to have much consequence, in hindsight, take on a much greater significance. My saying yes to Les was my 'Obama' moment.

The next 25 years or so were to be a fantastic experience for me and evoked so many wonderful memories and funny moments, which I hope to share with you. I hope this shows you a side of the film industry you never knew existed and gives you a few laughs on the way.

CHAPTER 2

MY FIRST DAY

As you would expect, Les was responsible for this. I didn't know anyone else who would give me a job, and he was becoming a bit like my mentor. He had a wealth of experience and was well thought of, and that is what I wanted to achieve.

Having parked my shiny Capri, I wandered onto the stage at Shepperton Studios in Middlesex to help on a remake of the film classic 'Thief of Baghdad', not really knowing what to expect. I was only booked for one day, and we were shooting a scene in the film in a giant eagle's nest where a four-foot egg hatches and the fluid inside pours out. Obviously, I hadn't done this before.

At a point of inactivity, while everyone was setting up, Les decided to visit the loo.

"Don't worry, there's nothing for us to do. Just hang around in case someone calls. But they won't," he had said.

He had barely gone two minutes when my worst fear was realised.

"Props!" shouted the First assistant.

My heart sank, and I frantically looked round, hoping Les

would magically emerge from the toilet. No such luck. Again, the First shouted. I couldn't ignore this, so I gathered myself and walked over to him.

"Yes... Props?" I said, trying to summon an air of confidence that I blatantly did not have.

"Where's Les?" he said.

"In the loo. Can I help? I'm his brother, Pete, and working with him today."

"Right! What are we doing with the egg?" he enquired as if I knew what he was talking about.

I tried to stall and act knowledgeable, but I had no idea.

"Which bit are we doing?" I was now getting into this.

"The cracking of the egg. What have you made up for the fluid coming out?"

I could feel his eyes boring into me, waiting for my reply.

There was a short answer to his question. Nothing, but I could hardly tell him that.

The Special effects department, which is so well known these days, was in its very early stages then, so the Props Department did all of this, and at this moment I was their sole representative who had no experience at all to draw on. I had to think of something quickly or look like a complete fool. What would look like egg fluid, run freely, and we could make up in large quantities?

The First was staring at me, I could feel myself getting quite hot, and then, as if all my stars had aligned and the Gods were on my side, words came involuntarily from my lips.

"Wallpaper paste!"

"Wallpaper paste," he echoed my words.

What had I said? He must think I'm an idiot.

"That's a great idea. Looks exactly like the inside of an egg," he said.

"Yes." I was convincing myself it was a good idea, almost as if I had planned it, which I obviously hadn't, so I went on with my brainchild.

"I thought with wallpaper paste, we could vary the flow of the fluid by making it thicker or thinner."

"Brilliant. Can't catch an old Prop Man out, can we?" he enthused.

If only he had known how easy it would have been to catch this Prop Man out, and he very nearly did.

"We do try." I smiled.

Wallpaper pastes for the uninitiated are small packets of flaky powder that, when mixed with warm water, make a sticky globular substance that is used to stick decorative wallpapers on the interior walls of your house. Not so popular these days, but quite the thing back then.

Les finally emerged on to the stage, and now I had to explain this to him. He had left me for a few minutes, and I had made this decision on my own without consulting him.

"Ok?" he said.

"Yes, but the First wanted to know what we have made up for the egg fluid," I replied.

He looked at me. 'What the hell have you said?' was written all over his face.

"What did you say?" He was clearly anxious.

It was done now, so no point in lying.

"Wallpaper paste!" I waited for the reaction.

He thought for a second, then finally said, "That's actually a good idea."

Thank God for that!

We did use it. Buckets and buckets of it, and it worked well. Even the Director commented on it. I felt fully vindicated with my decision until I realised I had forgotten we had to clear all the mess up afterward, and boy, was there a mess. Les and I were down on our knees with buckets of warm soapy water, trying to dilute the paste and rinse the floor for what seemed like an eternity. We thought we had done a good job but had to leave the floor to dry out. It was only after a couple of days that everyone realised there were still remnants of it all over the stage floor, and people's shoes were sticking to it like Velcro.

That was it! My first job as a Prop Man. I was buzzing and couldn't wait to get home and tell Ann. We sat and laughed at the money I had just earned for one day compared to what I had been earning. Our future had taken a turn for the better; although I didn't have another job to go to, but that wasn't the point, I had taken the first step.

CHAPTER 3

FIRST OBSERVATIONS

It's amazing, but after one job I felt I had learned so much. The first day in any career is always daunting and probably everyone remembers it vividly, and this was no different for me.

There was constant pressure throughout the day for all departments to get their part right, for it wasn't good enough for one to do well, we all had to do well and all at the same time, or nothing would work. That's why it was like a kind of family that came together for a fixed period, got it done, and then disappeared again.

I realised you had to prepare well, not to keep up with the game but, moreover, to keep ahead of it, for without preparation you could easily go under and some stories later in the book will illustrate this fully.

Preparing well almost became my Mantra, and as my career progressed, I would become almost fanatical about it, and I seemed almost drawn to those who saw things the same way as me and wary of those who didn't.

From a Prop Man's point of view, not being caught out involved having the right equipment to do the work, and throughout the years, the amount of stuff I carried just got bigger and bigger. Some other Prop Men even drove vans. My first day on set I had one toolbox and one bag, and looking at what Les had with him, I realised that was never going to be enough.

I also learned the hierarchy that existed on set, very much like what you might see in the animal world and taking on a rough Pyramid shape.

At the top would be the Producers who would look after the financing and other important far-ranging matters.

Then would be the Director. I think most people would understand his or her duties. They take the script, devour it and strive to see their vision reproduced on the big screen, particularly dealing with the cast.

Beneath these two levels, the Pyramid starts to spread into the various departments that all play their role in making it happen, and those are divided into heads of department, assistants, etc.

Between the Production and the general crew come the Assistants. The First rules on set, and everything goes through them, and they have one or two other assistants to help them enforce things.

On most films, you will see the same groupings that would include the Production department, which is there to make it all happen in its various forms, the Camera Department, The Lighting Department, The Art Department for the visual interpretation of the film and who work closely with the Construction and Props Departments to put their vision into practise. Then there would be Make-up and Hair, Wardrobe, Special Effects, Publicity, Catering, possibly Model-makers, etc.

The whole thing could involve hundreds of technicians, but everyone knows exactly where on the pecking order they are. When you look at the end-credits on a film next time, take a close look at the way they are set out. Those on their own are important, those in a long list are less important, and the further down the list you go, well, I don't need to explain.

Within my department you have The Prop Master, who is obviously in charge and works closely with the Art Department and Construction. Under him is a storeman who looks after all the props being hired or bought and sends them back when they are finished with. There is a dressing crew of varying numbers who 'dress' sets and then 'strike' them when they are finished, and finally there are the 'Standbys' who are constantly on set with the shooting crew to do anything that they need to do prop-wise, help with continuity, hand out props to artists and all those other jobs no one wants to do.

I soon learned where Prop Men were on this list. You were vital when your bit was necessary but very expendable when it started costing the Production money. The Prop Master might make it up the list, but those under him would not easily be seen, if at all. In all the films I worked on, and that was over 20 or so, I got very few credits, but it was nice to see my name on the ones where I did get recognised as being a contributory factor. Everyone working on a film is there for a reason, or they would not be on it, and I took solace in the fact that my small part was vital at that moment, and I should be proud of that. Credits were nice but not essential.

The one thing that was certain in my mind was that the Film industry was my future. I had dabbled in so many jobs in my life without ever finding something I thought I could truly make a career in, but now I had. It was unique and different in so many ways from anything I had done, and I resolved to do everything I needed to make this work for my family and me. At this point, all I could see were the benefits with no downside, but as my career unfolded, I realised I had been looking through those rose-tinted glasses a little too much.

CHAPTER 4

WHAT NEXT?

Other than Les and John, I didn't know anyone who would give me a job, so at first, I did odd days on films, mainly through Les, and this was mostly unloading and loading trucks, helping dress and strike sets and pack up props to return them to the hire companies. The bread and butter of propping.

During this time, I met other Prop Men, and the stories they told had me in fits. I could sit and listen to them for hours as one story led to another, then another, and in me they had a captive audience. It made the world I had entered even more exciting, and I couldn't wait for my own experiences to begin. I wouldn't have to wait long.

The network of getting work was beginning to work for me, and I began getting the occasional call from people I had hardly met, but probably who knew my name to be Benson, which would have helped. Thanks, Les.

This helped me in getting more work and, out of the blue, I was asked to do a full three weeks on a film called 'The Corn is Green' which starred the legendary Katharine Hepburn, who was in her seventies then, and was directed by George

Cukor, who directed over 30 films himself. He was even older than Katharine, but they had been friends for years and had worked on 10 films together.

My part was helping with dressing and striking, but very often I ventured on to set and got glimpses of these greats at work. I was a man of nearly 30 but felt like a kid in a sweet-shop watching all of this. I was truly in awe. One day as I was watching, Katharine had finished and was walking off set when an object barred her way. I got a beaming smile from her as I moved it out of the way. Silly, I know, but I always remember that moment I came face to face with a true legend of movies.

That meeting had more effect on me than I realised at that moment, for that fleeting smile from a true Hollywood great made me realise I wanted more than just dressing and striking sets; I wanted to be part of the shooting crew, so I was determined to become a Standby and meet and work with all these famous people.

This had been the first time I had been away for more than a day or so, and during the week I had stayed with Les at his house in Borehamwood in Hertfordshire, not far from Twickenham studios where we were filming, and then gone home at the weekend. It was a strange feeling coming back on a Friday night, staying for two days and then driving away again for a week. Ann was on her own and heavily pregnant, although she did have two sisters who lived close by, and it didn't feel right leaving her, but we needed the money with our family about to expand, so it was Catch 22.

I decided that after this, I would stop taking any work until our first baby was born, and when my job was finished, I headed home fully intent on sticking to my promise, but I had only been there a matter of hours when the phone rang, and I was offered a three-day job. Not on a film this time, but on a commercial, something I had never done before, and I didn't even know who had put my name forward. The money was even better than films, but it meant I would have to standby for the first time, which was a truly daunting prospect.

Ann and I discussed it and decided that as this was only three days away from home and she wasn't due for another couple of weeks, I should take the work. I would be home well before the birth and help where I could. I wasn't really prepared for what that 'help' might entail, but I'm sure I would find out soon.

On the day, I got up very early and drove straight to Shepperton, where the commercial was being shot. For the two nights I was away, I had planned to stay with my mum and dad in Borehamwood rather than drive up and down.

This was a French company shooting French shoes and, for what they planned to do, I wondered why they had even bothered to come to England. They hadn't even brought the shoes they were going to shoot on and decided it was my job to go out with a bundle of money and find them for them. This wasn't my job, but maybe in France this was the way they did it, so off I went, armed with some photos of shoes I had to match to.

I was surprised how straightforward this had been, and I was sure I had bought all they may need, so I decided to try to find a phone and let them know the situation. Remember, there were no mobiles then.

They seemed pleased but said it was late now, so not to bother coming back. They would see me in the morning.

It was great seeing Mum and Dad again, but I was tired and had an early start, so I was in bed by 10 and fast asleep when at 3.30am, Mum's phone rang. Mum knocked on the bedroom door and said it was Ann's sister, Lin.

She told me not to panic, though she didn't seem so calm herself, but Ann had gone into labour early and been taken to Ashford hospital in Kent. I had to go, but I had all the shoes and spare cash still with me, and they were needed at the studio in a few hours' time. Mum said she would put them all in a taxi and get them to the studio for me. Just get in the car and drive and phone the French producer later to explain.

I hoped the 'Road Gods' would be with me on my journey and get me there in time, so I put my foot to the floor and hit the road. The drive back was a blur, but every red light turned to green when it was required and, eventually at around 6am, I slid into the hospital car park. Absolutely knackered and hoping I was in time, I raced down the corridors to the Maternity ward.

Ann was sitting up in bed, and there were no new additions to be seen, so incredibly, I had made it. More incredible was that just 10 minutes later, Ann was in the delivery room, and our first baby, Ellenna, was born. She was beautiful.

Later, Ann said she had been trying to hold on until I got there, and when she heard the row of someone running down a corridor, she realised it was me and relaxed. Amazing!

Caught up in the Euphoria of the moment, I'd clearly forgotten all about the shoes and calling the Producer, so I had to find a phone and explain. Naively, I thought she would understand and congratulate us, but all I got was a line of abuse and called unprofessional. No one was going to spoil this day, so I took this all in, took a deep breath and told her that I would not be invoicing her for the job, so she had my services for free and to have a good life. I think that's what I said.

I never worked for that company again, which was no surprise, and still, I hadn't 'stood-by', but I was now a father, very proud to be one, and there was even more reason to make my career work.

I didn't get any more calls for commercials, nor did I crave them, as I much preferred to make my way in films, but for the present, I wanted to be with my newly expanded family and let the future sort itself out.

Ellie settled into a lovely routine quite quickly, and it was great being home to see it, but a new addition means more costs and with no money coming in, the pressure to find work mounted. The money from the French commercial would have helped, but that was water under the bridge now, so I had to find new work, which wasn't easy. I had to wait patiently and believe it would happen when it was ready.

CHAPTER 5

THE BREAKTHROUGH

Eventually, the phone rang, but it was only a one-day job helping the dressing crew on a film called 'The Stud', starring Joan Collins. It was a routine day and welcomed for the financial side, but it was the timing of this day that led to a real watershed moment for me and helped shape my future.

My mentor, Les, was obviously involved and was there with me on the day, together with another Prop Man I hadn't met before, Arthur Wicks. He was nice and liked a good laugh, so the day went by easily, but the importance of him being there was far greater, for he was to be the Prop Master on a TV series called 'The Professionals' starting the following year in March. It was about spies, MI5, etc., and starred Gordon Jackson, Martin Shaw and Lewis Collins and ran for 9 months in production, churning out an episode every two weeks. Seat of your pants stuff!

It goes without saying that he had asked Les if he wanted to standby on it, and Les had hedged his bets, saying he had some other things going on and would let him know nearer the time. A dangerous strategy, but if you were established, you could make these sorts of calls. I wasn't, but would have ripped his hand off if he had asked me.

To his credit, Les told Arthur that if he didn't do it, then he was sure I would. He was certainly right there. If that happened, it would be the first time I had started a full production in my own right, a truly wonderful thought. My head was spinning, but it was a slim chance, so I had to sit and wait it out.

This was my first year, and I didn't know how work went in any one year, so with a new daughter and feeling tired, I took my foot off the pedal and found myself in December having done very little work. Having spoken to Les, I realised new work wasn't abundant at this time of year and, unless you were already on something, didn't pick up until around March. March! Our finances wouldn't stretch that far.

Here was another lesson learned. Never say no to anything unless you have another sure-fired job to go to, whatever it is, as you are as good as your last job.

Six months I was out of work. We had spent all the money I had made, and I had a family to support. A feeling of desperation was starting to take hold. Folkestone was hardly the hub of the Film industry, and not many productions came unless they were lost. The local papers didn't offer any solutions, so reluctantly, I signed on at the Job Centre, something I told myself I would never do.

Here at least, this Government Organisation would pass on suitable work to you when it was available, and every week you had to come in, 'sign on' and, for this, you would get a small amount of money to help tide you over. Not much, but it helped.

I remember sitting in the office at my 'induction', trying to explain to the lady conducting the interview what my work entailed. She clearly was not versed in the workings of the Film industry and had no idea what I was talking about.

"What is the name of your job?" she asked.

"I am a Prop Man," I replied

"Prop Man." I heard her mouthing the words as she wrote them down on her form.

"We have nothing on the books at the moment, but we will let you know if anything comes in."

The chances of that phone call ever being made seemed extremely unlikely, but for 5 weeks I turned up on a Tuesday at 9.45 am to 'sign on'. Never likely to be offered an 'appropriate' job.

In the meantime, I had been selling bits and pieces and making small rattan furniture, which was trendy at the time, just to make ends meet.

Then, one morning, the phone did ring, and it was the Job Centre offering me a job that had just come in and would I come in to discuss it. Would I? You bet I would. I wondered what it could be. Maybe a Film company on location needing extra labour, which would have been great, so I couldn't get to the office quickly enough.

"You'll be pleased to know that we have found you some appropriate work as a Prop Man," the lady said.

"What is it, a film or a commercial?" I eagerly enquired.

"No, it's a travelling circus."

There was silence. She was serious.

"Doing what?" I almost shouted.

"Putting up the wood prop in the middle of the tent," she said matter-of-factly.

"But I have no idea how to do that. I could kill someone," I replied.

"Are you refusing appropriate work?" she said in an official capacity.

"No, I am refusing inappropriate work that I have never done in my life before and which could be dangerous to all concerned," I said in a raised voice.

"If you turn down what is deemed appropriate work by the department, then I will have to 149 you," she stormed back.

"149 me? What does that even mean?" I asked.

"It means your payments will be stopped for 6 weeks," she smugly said.

I was furious.

"Then you had better bloody 149 me, because there is no way I am doing that." I rose and stormed out of the office.

What was I going to do? The money wasn't a lot, but at least it was regular, and now there wasn't even that.

Christmas had been a low-key affair, but we had just about gotten through; now we had no income at all, so for the next few months I did absolutely anything to make money. I worked on a lathe in a garage, grinding out crankshafts for cars. I had no clue what I was doing. I drove a van all over the Southeast of England, delivering engines. I did painting and decorating. I did stocktaking in a small local company. You name it; I probably had a go at it. The heady days of the film industry seemed a distant memory. I had almost forgotten that I was a Prop Man any more. Ann tried to boost my moral saying something would turn up, but what?

Then one evening the phone rang.

"Hello, is that Pete?" the voice said.

"Yes, who's this?" I replied.

"It's Arthur Wicks. Don't know if you remember me? We did a day together on 'The Stud' with your brother."

I certainly did remember that name.

"I was wondering if you would like to be standby on 'The Professionals' starting in March at Wembley Studios for six months or maybe more?" he went on.

If he had been there, I would have kissed him.

"Yes, I would. That would be great. Thanks for asking," I said as casually as I could.

"Perfect! I did ask Les, but he had something else on, so I thought I'd ask you," said Arthur.

"I am glad you did. Grateful for the call," I said.

"That's fine," he said. "I've just finished on a production.

Had a busy time of it. What have you been doing?"

He really did not want to know.

"Bits and pieces. Nice to be on a run again," I lied.

"Ok, I'll call you nearer the time." Arthur rang off.

I put the phone down and looked at Ann. I don't know who was more relieved, but now, at least, this nightmare was over. We opened our last bottle of wine and boy did it taste good.

March was still some time off, and we still had to scramble to make a living, but now we had a purpose.

Finally, the breakthrough!

CHAPTER 6

THE PROFESSIONALS

Walking down a seedy street in the East end of London, Bodie and Doyle spot their suspect. He spots them. They exchange glances, and the chase begins. Down streets and alleyways, the pursuit gathers momentum. Bodie and Doyle are gaining on him, and he knows it is only a matter of time before he will be caught. In a last-ditch attempt to escape, he darts into a tenement building with the two boys close behind him, up a flight of stairs and into a corridor that has no way out except through a closed window. Briefly, he hesitates and looks back. Be caught or smash his way through the window? He chooses the latter and crashes through, jumping down on to the pavement below. Bodie and Doyle stand in disbelief, look down at the drop and decide with knowing glances that the chase is over.

Another scene from the hit British TV series of the 1970s, 'The Professionals'. This was the world I was now about to enter as my first attempt at standing by on a full production. In the days before starting, I was a bag of nerves. I hadn't worked on a film for months and felt I'd forgotten how to do it, and this time I was a Standby on a full production, so to say

I didn't get much sleep is an understatement.

I was going to be away from home for a longer period than I had ever been before, and once again I had to stay up during the week, this time at Les's house in Borehamwood. I didn't know a soul on this apart from a brief working day with Arthur, so I took a deep breath and walked into the Prop Room, hoping for the best.

After a few introductions, Arthur gave me a script for the first episode we would shoot the next week. My first script. This was a first. Wish I had kept it.

"Read that, break it down and let me know if you might need anything," Arthur said.

I sat and read it, often going over bits trying to find something, anything that no one else might have thought of, but it all looked fine to me. There again, I had no experience with this, so it would probably look fine. I began to wonder if this was a test. Obvious paranoia setting in.

Finally, enough was enough, and I put the script down.

"I can't find anything unusual in there," I pronounced to Arthur and waited for his reaction.

"Yes, it's quite straightforward this one," replied Arthur.

Inwardly, there was a big sigh as if I had just passed an exam at school.

I spent the next couple of days loading our Prop truck which would be with us at all times, carrying everything we might need for the shoot. In charge was my fellow standby, Paul Hedges. A fair few of his relatives were also Prop Men, but so far, I hadn't encountered any of them, and as I went through my career, I found this wasn't uncommon in families. Look at Les and me, for instance.

He was a really nice funny man, but I sensed that education hadn't been a big part of his life and use of the English language was sketchy. This was no more illustrated than when we were seeing in the props for the first episode, and a folding wheelchair had been delivered.

"That must be for the dishevelled gentleman," he proudly pronounced.

I couldn't help myself and burst out laughing. I thought he was joking, but his face said otherwise. It was just me laughing.

"What?" He genuinely looked hurt.

"Sorry, you know what dishevelled means, don't you? It means someone down on their luck, a bit unkempt, untidy. You're thinking of a disabled gentleman." I waited.

Now he got it. Now we both laughed. At that moment, I think I realised we would work well together for the next six months or so.

The day before our first shooting day, I got a call sheet. Once again, a first for me, and I never kept that either. It listed everything that was going on that day, the crew, catering, locations, and most importantly, the shot numbers we planned to do that day.

Now, I was inexperienced, but I had seen call sheets before, and they had about 6 to 8 shots per day to do. This had 46. 46!

I asked Arthur if that was a mistake.

He told me each episode took about two 5-day weeks to shoot, which produced around an hour of TV time. If we hadn't done it by then, a small second unit picked them up and finished the episode. In TV, there was no money in the budget for take after take, and a lot of the shots were people running, close-ups, etc., so they ripped through the shots very quickly. This isn't 'Star Wars' we're doing here; this is cheapo TV productions to fill up TV slots, he had said.

Well, there's my bubble burst.

After the first days of shooting, I could see what he meant. Every shot was no more than 3 or 4 takes, and then move on fast. No one seemed to care about quality if they had a shot that would string a sequence together and would finish an episode. Getting to know the crew, I began to see that many of them were doing the same as me. They, in their own way, were just as green as I was, and were using this type of work to hone their skills for bigger projects. Nothing wrong with that; it also made me feel a whole lot better about myself and was also giving me a regular income that I hadn't had for months. No complaints there.

The three main artists in this were Gordon Jackson, Martin Shaw and Lewis Collins, and all had their own personalities, which differed greatly.

Gordon was a true 'Gent', extremely polite and genuinely interested when he spoke to you. He'd had a long career in acting and been in many films, done theatre, the lot. I wondered why he ever took this role, for it seemed a bit below his ability. Must have had his reasons.

Martin was a bit of a pin-up boy with long curly locks and a huge following of young female fans. He was vegan and deep into keeping fit. Trying to look after his needs in food shots was challenging sometimes; where in one scene, I had to yellow food dye some cottage cheese to make it look like scrambled eggs which, as a vegan, he couldn't eat.

Lewis was a bit of a firebrand and was constantly at loggerheads with the producer, Ray Menmuir, often threatening to walk off set. I lost count of the number of times Ray had to talk him down and get the shooting going again.

A funny example of this was on an extremely fraught day of shooting when Lewis was in a foul mood. It wasn't going to take much to set him off. Not sure what it was that started him, but he kicked off, and Ray was called.

I had best mention that when Ray was younger, he had an accident and lost two fingers on his right hand. It didn't prevent him doing anything normal, but on this day, it was to be highlighted. The dispute between the two became heated, and it looked as if Lewis would actually leave this time.

"You are not leaving until we have this shot," Ray told Lewis.

"Really? Who's going to stop me? You?" Lewis said defiantly.

"Yes. Me!" replied Ray, standing his ground.

Without thinking about what he was saying, Lewis blurted out. "What, are you going to hit me with a bunch of threes?" Referring to Ray's hand.

For those of you unfamiliar with the expression, it is a bunch of fives, meaning a hand with five fingers on it, like a bunch of bananas.

For a split second, there was silence on the set. This was deeply personal to Ray, but he took it in his stride and hit back.

"No, Lewis. I'm left-handed, so it will be the full five!"

Everyone laughed, and the situation was defused. Ray had done what every producer needed to do and kept the production running. He went up in my estimations that day.

One incident that sticks in my mind and illustrates exactly what I was saying about the budget and the restraints on production it caused came on a day when the sequence was Martin and Lewis chasing a suspect. They pursue him into a disused building and up a flight of stairs, and when the suspect finds himself cornered in a dead-end corridor, he throws himself through a closed window to escape.

Stunts are a tricky thing to pull off, and the services of a professional stunt arranger are almost always used. This sequence couldn't be done safely in the building we were first in, so they had the Construction reproduce a mocked-up set in a park, so we had total control over it.

A stunt man was brought in to perform the action, and Paul and I made up a pile of cardboard stunt boxes and covered them in mattresses, so he had something soft to fall on. I have to say this guy was one hell of a poser, arriving on set wearing just a small pair of 'Speedo' swimming trunks and a pair of trainers to reveal his perfect tan. He was an instant hit amongst the crew.

The window he was to smash through was made of the thinnest wood and cut in so many places you wondered how it was still in one piece, but we only had one of them. Yes, one!

If you tried this with a real window, I guarantee you wouldn't get very far, and every time I see this sort of action in a film, I have never thought it looked right, but here we were again trying to convince the viewer.

We had 3 cameras on this at different angles to cover every eventuality, and checks were being made repeatedly until the First was satisfied we were ready. Finally, he asked the cameras to roll and then shouted those famous words, "Action!"

The stunt man ran, threw himself at the window, which didn't fully give way, so he was now stuck half in and half out and wondering what to do next. You can imagine the thoughts running through his mind at that moment, and his decision, rightly or wrongly, was to wrestle himself free and perform a theatrical-style forward roll on to his crash mats.

The cry of 'Cut' rang out from the First as everyone, for a split second, stood staring in amazement at what they had just witnessed.

Ray Menmuir's face said what everyone was thinking. We had one chance to do this, and that was the result we got for all the preparations. To my mind it looked unusable, and on bigger films we would have gone again, maybe even a few more times, but we didn't have that luxury, and we also had another 40 or so shots to do that day.

"Right, let's move on," said the director to mostly everybody's surprise, and that's exactly what we did as if we were satisfied with it. The truth of the matter was we had to be satisfied with it because we didn't have the budget to do anything about it. They must have found a way round it in post-production because that episode can be found in the series, but it did illustrate what I was saying about this type of production.

The filming went on at this ridiculous pace for well over six months, working a manic schedule, but eventually the last shot was in the can, and we now had the full Series 3 of 'The Professionals.'

I had completed my first full production, and if I am honest, although it was absolute pandemonium at times and sometimes 'un-Professional', I had learned an awful lot. I felt that my career was settling down, although I was completely exhausted and dying to get back to see my family and spend time with them. Turning up at weekends shattered and not really wanting to say much I was so tired, hardly helped things. We needed time to return to normal again because when you are apart so much you can't put your life on hold, so you act like a single person again.

Fortunately, money wise we were ok, and I was able to be at home for a while and spend time with Ann and Ellenna. It was a great feeling looking at the two of them, knowing I was now gaining the ability to properly look after them, and our lives could only improve because of it.

I took a few odd jobs here and there, which kept the money topped up, but it was another full film I was craving. I had loved being on set with the main unit and being in the centre of it all, meeting new people, meeting all the stars. This is what I wanted for me, but that was out of my hands, and it was so frustrating knowing that.

I wondered if that would ever change.

CHAPTER 7
FINDING WORK

The whole set up of the film industry made finding your next job quite unpredictable. The people at the top would always feature in the film's publicity and get known because of it. Their wares, so to speak, would be on show to the whole world, and work would be offered to them because of it. The lower down the ranks you went, the more invisible you became, and you were one of many vying for the same job. We all had our home commitments, and we all had to keep finding work to service those commitments, so it became a dog-eat-dog existence with the winner coming out on top.

The means by which the likes of myself got work was determined by several factors.

You could be in an existing established crew with a popular Prop Master who got loads of work, and subsequently, so did you. You were lucky to be in this position, but it did mean you had to 'stay in' with that Prop Master and do all the films he wanted. If you turned one down, you might fall out of sync and never work with them again.

You could sit on a phone for hours calling all the Prop Masters you heard might have a chance on a film and pretend to be their best friend.

You could put your name down on the Union Register for Prop Men seeking employment, but unfortunately it didn't have a good name and could often be detrimental to your career.

You could try the old-fashioned way and work hard, try to do well, get noticed and build your reputation for being reliable.

Another option at this time was to tour the bars at all the studios and see who was in there and 'socialise' yourself into a job. I can't tell you how many people at all levels obtained work through this method, strange as it may seem.

At this time, drink driving laws were very lax in the UK. Although breathalysers had been around since 1938, the first one being called 'The Drunkometer', they were not widely used and amazingly, although drunk driving was a motoring offence since the 1960s, it didn't become a criminal offence until 1988. So the film industry, for one, didn't take much notice of such things. They drank, staggered to their cars and saw six lines in the middle of the road on the way home. Thank God we changed all that.

I never got any work like this, but that's not to say it wasn't fruitful, and you could see this so well shown in the next film I worked on called "The Elephant Man". While I was at Wembley on 'The Professionals', I met a Prop Master called Terry Wells. He also, as I mentioned previously with Paul, had other relatives who were Prop Men. We got speaking because he knew Les very well. Who didn't?

He mentioned he had this film coming up and was looking for crew, so I casually mentioned I would be available if he needed someone, not really expecting much to come of it.

Just when I was settling into home life again, Terry phoned, offering me a job. I couldn't believe it, but working on my idea not to turn any work down, I accepted.

It was a period drama starring John Hurt, who had to undergo hours of Prosthetics every day just to be able to act his part, and we had a lot of arduous dressing in old disused hospitals.

To cut a long story short, my drinking habits fell well short of the expectations of my fellow Prop Men, who clearly knew the insides of Wembley bar as a hunting ground for new work, and I think Terry rather enjoyed the social side of things and went along with their visions. I stayed with the film, but I was never going to be part of Terry's permanent crew and, as it turned out, Fate had a better route for me to take.

Les had been offered a job as a Standby on a film, but he didn't really like that role and preferred to be on the dressing crew, which still left the Prop Master needing to fill that position, so after my vast experience on The Professionals, Les put my name forward.

Out of the blue I got a call from Tony Teiger, the Prop Master, offering me a job on 'The Mirror Crack'd', the film I mentioned at the beginning of my book. I was really excited to get started.

CHAPTER 8

THE MIRROR CRACK'D

Elizabeth Taylor frantically throws clothes into her suitcases as Rock Hudson enters her bedroom and asks what she is doing.

"Someone is trying to kill me; I am so scared. I need to get out of here," she screams. Rock crosses the room and throws his arms around her as she bursts into floods of tears. He knows the truth, but doesn't want to show it.

The camera stays on their faces as they are both deep in their own thoughts.

We are back on the set of 'The Mirror Crack'd'. Another scene unfolds between two of the big stars of this film, which was such a memorable film for me in more ways than one. Although I stood by on 'The Professionals', it was only for television, whereas this was my first time as a Standby on a full feature film that would be shown worldwide and had a cast to die for.

I was also to get to know some of the cast on a more personal basis that no one could have foreseen, as you will see as the story unfolds.

The film was an Angela Lansbury 'Miss Marple' whodunnit about an American film company that comes to shoot in Miss Marple's sleepy little village of St Mary Mead, with the obvious murder twist.

Apart from interior shots at Twickenham Studios in Middlesex, a lot of shooting was based in a huge country estate just outside Sevenoaks in Kent.

Following the usual pattern, the Stars and Bigwigs were put in large expensive hotels close to the location, where we lesser mortals were billeted in local pubs close by, but our Pub was really nice and friendly, so it was no problem at all.

On the first day of shooting, I found myself rubbing shoulders with some of the biggest named actors and actresses around at that time. It was hard to take in that someone of my background would be having a cup of tea outside a country estate with the likes of Tony Curtis, Rock Hudson, Angela Lansbury, etc, but this was a reality, and I felt extremely fortunate to be there.

Elizabeth Taylor had not arrived yet, and for me, this was the person I most wanted to meet. Her life had been portrayed in the papers as being full of turmoil and problems, and I just wanted to see for myself what she was actually like.

I didn't have to wait long, for a few days later a small cavalcade of cars arrived carrying Elizabeth and what seemed like an army of PAs, hairdressers, make-up artists, wardrobe assistants, etc. I would not have been surprised if there wasn't a plumber in there as well; there were so many people.

The Second Assistant fought his way through the crowd of hangers-on and directed her towards the set, with her entourage following close behind. She could hardly move with the melee of helpers surrounding her. She, indeed, had a presence that made you wary of approaching her without permission, and this was how it was on set.

Elizabeth would arrive, get fussed over by her 'people', do her bit and leave the set having hardly said a word to anyone barring the Director, Guy. The atmosphere was not great, and I think even Elizabeth wasn't keen either, but I suppose she had been through this a hundred times and was a true professional, so on we went.

Part of my duties as a standby is to hand artists their props when required, and this day I had to hand one to Elizabeth, and I felt nervous in doing so. I handed her the prop but felt I should say something friendly so it didn't look so clinical and found myself asking her if she was enjoying being back in England again. She looked visibly surprised, and for a moment I thought I had overstepped the mark.

"It's nice. Thanks for asking. I didn't think anyone was talking to me," she said.

"No, it's not that. It's just difficult with all of your helpers around you," I tried to explain.

"Is that the problem?" she replied, obviously turning it over in her mind.

I just smiled and walked off.

The next day on set, Elizabeth arrived with no entourage at all. She had banished them and would call them only if she needed them. It was as if she could finally breathe, and from that moment she was a different person, clearly enjoying the interaction with the crew as she hadn't before.

We got on well and often exchanged a few words between shots, and then one day, as we were coming up to the weekend, I asked her what she was going to do with her days off. Apparently, a dinner party was being held by the owner of the Estate for top production personnel and the 'Stars'. Simple plebes like me were not invited.

"That'll be nice," I said.

"No, it will be extremely boring. Rock and I don't want to go. We're dreading it," she replied.

"What are you doing?" she went on.

I told her that Roy, the other Standby, was having a birthday party in the pub we were staying in, so probably a few drinks were in order.

"That sounds a lot of fun. I'd much prefer that to sitting with this stuffy lot pretending to enjoy it." She almost sounded envious.

"Well, at least your acting talents will come in useful there," I joked.

She smiled with an expression that seemed as if she would like to be invited. Surely not! The words were out of my mouth before I could stop them.

"Why don't you come, and Rock if he wants to?"

You could see she was actually contemplating the idea, but smiled and said, "Don't think that would go down well with the powers that be, do you?"

"Probably not. Anyway, the invite is there should you change your mind. We'll be there from about 8 o'clock onwards."

That night in the pub, we started drinking quite early, and the party was beginning to get moving. I had been having my leg pulled about inviting them. It did seem a bit far-fetched they would take me up on it, but about a quarter to nine, the pub door opened and in walked Liz and Rock. I hadn't seen them enter, but one of the other Prop Men had and shouted for me to go and meet them.

I was more surprised than anyone, but they were standing, wondering what to do, so I rushed over and ushered them to our table like a mother hen. We got them a drink, and within no time we were sitting round the table chatting as if we were old friends. They looked totally relaxed and were great fun to talk to. Unfortunately, every good thing comes to an end, and this was no exception. Other people in the pub had noticed them, and word was spreading fast round the village that the local had celebrities in their midst. The pub started to get more crowded as people flocked in to see Liz and Rock. Then the first autograph hunter plucked up the courage to approach, followed by more and more would-be collectors. Cameras appeared from nowhere, and the whole situation was descending into chaos. They had most likely experienced this so many times that they took it in their stride, but they had left their relaxed state and returned to protective mode. Within ten minutes, they said they had to go and thanked us all for a lovely time. Their car arrived, and they were whisked away. For half an hour they had been free, but now they were public property again.

I realised then that sometimes being one of the invisible plebs did have its advantages. I could drink in any pub in the world, and no one would care. They didn't have that freedom. They had fame and wealth, and I wondered if sometimes they would give that all up just to go back to being normal.

Monday morning, we arrived back on set. I couldn't wait to ask what had happened after they left the pub, but I didn't get a chance, for Tony was there to greet us with a face like a sore bum. Liz and Rock arrived at the dinner two hours late, which didn't go down well with the hosts, the other cast and production.

They were even less pleased to find out they went to the Props party instead on my invite. Tony had got it in the ear, and he was now passing that on to us in no small amount. He said it would have tarnished his reputation and lost him further work, and it was all down to me. Off his Christmas list, then.

When Liz and Rock did come on set, they did have a bit of a smirk on their faces, and we exchanged a secret smile, but I like to think they enjoyed themselves, however brief a moment.

As I relay this story after so many years, it is so surreal that I sometimes wonder if I imagined all this, but a chance encounter some 30 years later with a Solar panels salesman in my home in Kent put me straight.

As we were considering putting panels on our roof, we had a salesman come round to give us a quote. We were chatting, and he asked what I did for a living. I told him I was retired, but I used to work in the film industry. Inevitably he asked if I had met any famous people and, as we were in Kent, the story about Elizabeth came to mind. I started to tell the details about the pub in a village just outside Sevenoaks when he interrupted me.

"Funnily enough, I had a mate who used to live over that way, and he was sitting in a pub one night when in walks Elizabeth Taylor and Rock Hudson," he said.

I hadn't mentioned Rock's name at all, but he was describing the exact same night. What were the chances of this conversation happening over 30 years after the event? One thing, though; it did prove I hadn't made it up.

That film has always stuck with me for being my first feature film as a Standby, meeting so many well-known people and spending a short spell having a pint in a local with Liz and Rock, an experience I will never forget. Who wouldn't want a memory like that and so I thought it was a fitting way to start my book.

It's a shame the film wasn't more successful, and even Angela Lansbury herself said it was dreadful apparently, and she was one of the leading actresses. Need I say more?

For me, it was a raging success, but I don't think Tony ever forgave me, as I didn't work with him much after that. I waited for my next job to come along, which was to come via Les again. I have mentioned Les many times throughout without telling you much about him, so this is probably a good time to do just that.

CHAPTER 9
MY BROTHER LES

Les was my one and only brother, being three years older than me and had always looked after me from an early age. I had gone through the whole English education system, finally ending up with a Bachelor of Arts degree at a London University. Les had left school when he was 16 years old and gone to work in a local DIY shop, which he hated, but he didn't have a lot of choices. He would have done the same as me as he was very intelligent, but we had emigrated to Canada, and through an illness to our grandmother had returned, putting Les totally out of sync with the English system and giving him no time to learn enough to pass a vital exam which would have put him on the same path I took.

That was not going to deter him, as he was a very able and resourceful person who would achieve whatever he set out to do. This shop job would never define him, and as we lived in a town with a major film studio in it, namely MGM studios, he applied and got a job, being in a pool of workers who were told each day by the Studio what they would be doing that day.

They were assigned to various departments, such as the plasterers, the carpenters, the stagehands, and the props, without having the skills for any of them. One wonders how that ever worked, but that's what their system was. Les preferred the Prop department and did all he could to stay in it.

What was coming to his aid was a major shift in the way Studios were changing their operational mode. Their 'in-house' style of employment simply did not work and was costing them huge amounts of money for not a great return. Within a short time, the whole system went mostly 'freelance' where anyone needed was hired in on a short-term contract, only to be fired when the production was over.

For being in the right place at the right time, Les had become one of the first freelance Prop Men in the country and set the standards for all those who followed. A true pioneer of the industry.

It was no wonder he had a good name and was well known by so many, and was offered and worked on some of the biggest films being made at that time. As I was growing up, he was away a great deal of the time in so many exotic places that if I had kept all the postcards, I would have a vast collection by now.

He worked hard and played hard, but was very clever with his money and bought his own house at a very early age. He didn't like to owe anyone anything and was secretive about what he was doing, preferring to keep his affairs to himself.

He always looked after his family, even helping Mum and Dad financially when they bought their bungalow after they retired, but his marriages never went the way they were supposed to, and he never got to have his own children, who he would have spoilt rotten.

Sadly, he died at the ridiculously young age of 59, and I so miss him as he was so supportive of me and shaped my life in many ways.

We did have our arguments, as brothers always do, and

our different personalities showed in the way these tiffs went. Les was aggressively straightforward, whereas I tended to be a bit more diplomatic, as I found that worked better for me. As we got older, we did move further apart and did less and less socially, but there were some internal family matters that didn't help the situation, either.

Nevertheless, I loved him dearly despite our differences, and I wish he was still here to read this book, but as I said earlier, he was still playing a huge part in my job prospects and put my name forward to a Prop Master named George Ball, who was doing a film out of Elstree Studios in Hertfordshire called 'The Great Muppet Caper'. This was a Jim Henson film with all the 'Muppets' that everyone knows so well.

By chance, Les's house backed right on to this studio, and you could literally see the Prop room George was in from Les's window over the fence. The film was quite a long run, and Les had offered to let me stay at his house during the week and then drive home at the weekends, so the Sunday before I was supposed to start, I drove up to his house.

The problem was I had an almighty cold that was making me feel dreadful, and if I hadn't had this job would probably have stayed in my bed. Working for George was a huge break for me, and if I could pull it off and stay with him, it would change my career immensely. He was one of the best in the industry, if not the best, and was offered nearly everything going. If he took a film, it was generally a big-budget one and well paid, and he did one after another. To be a part of that would be a massive step for me, so I did not want to blow my first day.

I arrived at Les's house. When he saw me, he said how awful I looked, which made me feel so much better, but he said he had some medicine that might help and gave me something called 'Benylin'. I don't know if this is a product known throughout the world, but it's supposed to help colds. However, it is lethal and basically knocks you out so you can rest.

I had to be in the Prop room at 8 am on the Monday, so I took the medicine, set my alarm for 7 am and went to bed. This stuff certainly worked its magic, and I was out for the count. I slept straight through the alarm and then drowsily opened my eyes to see the clock read 7.55am, 5 minutes before I was supposed to be impressing the man who could change my life.

I have never dressed so fast in my life and, in a half stupor, found myself scrambling over the dividing fence. To go round to the main gate would take another 10 minutes I could ill afford, so I just went for it and staggered into the Prop room 10 minutes late and hardly knowing where I was. I had obviously made a great first impression with George, as he said.

"Nice of you to turn up. Good night, was it?"

"God, I wish it had been. I took 'Benylin', and it has completely wiped me out. I'm so sorry I am late," I tried to explain.

"Did you have to come far?" George enquired.

I couldn't say 100 metres, which would have been the truth, so I lied.

"Folkestone."

"You've done well. What time did you leave?" George went on.

"Oh, early." I could feel my nose growing longer as I said it.

I don't know if he ever believed me, but he was very supportive, and I found out that if you worked hard for him, he was very loyal to you. I didn't know it then, but George, like Les, would play a huge role in the rest of my career.

Now I had to get to grips with the task ahead. My first day with the Muppets.

CHAPTER 10

THE GREAT MUPPET CAPER

We pan over several beautiful swimmers posing around a pool in elaborate pink and purple bathing costumes as they swim. What you'll notice is how stark they are against the plain background. What you won't notice are the piles of heavy benches, palm trees, and my blood lying about 3 metres below all that.

This is the swimming pool set in which Miss Piggy performs with other muppets as synchronised swimmers in a scene from the film. The set had been dressed lavishly by the Prop Men and Art Department with the benches, trees and other large items which had to be manhandled up flights of man-made steps and put together by the riggers (scaffolders), but the Director, Jim Henson, had decided he didn't want any of this, and it all had to go down the steps again, which were now slippery from the swimmers performing.

All the other Prop Men were busy, so it was left to me and the other Standby, Denis Hopperton, to move all of this, which on our own would have taken hours. The First, in an effort to get this done, had enlisted everyone capable to help us clear the set.

This was fine in principle, but if you are not used to picking up and moving heavy, cumbersome objects down a flight of steep scaffold stairs, which are now wet and slippery, then it can become quite dangerous.

Everyone was getting involved, and I found myself waiting for someone to take the end of one of the benches. One of the assistants arrived to help, but we were a total mismatch. He was over 6 ft 2 inches tall, and I was a mere 5ft 8 inches. As we moved off with the bench, it was certainly at a very jaunty angle as we approached the stairs.

Feeling a moment of impending doom, I told the assistant to take it slowly and to let me guide us down the stairs. I might as well have been speaking Swahili, for he took no notice of what I just said and lifted his end up, transferring the whole load onto me. The sudden thrust threw me off balance, and my footing went, sending me backwards down the stairs with the huge bench following me. It wedged me at the bottom and took a fair few people to lift it off me. I sat for a moment, waiting for the inevitable pain to start, but surprisingly I felt nothing. I couldn't believe my luck. As I rose, someone said there was blood on my hand, and I looked down to see that my little finger had been split open like a pea with the impact of the bench.

Half an hour later, I was in A&E having treatment. Fortunately, there was no major damage, but it was a few weeks before I could play the piano again, which was uncanny, as I couldn't play it before!

That little finger never looked the same after that, but it became an old 'war wound' story for the grandchildren.

That whole incident illustrated what the audience never sees when they are watching the film.

We had to accommodate all the needs of the 'muppeteers' who sometimes had two or maybe three of them operating one muppet, depending on the action, and it was fascinating to see how it was all done. Things that could easily be carried by a human, for example, could not be carried by a muppet, so all special props had to be made. All the muppets were up in the air with the muppeteers below, so all the sets had to be constructed to accommodate this. Certainly, a new way of working for me, but great experience.

One other lasting memory I had from this film was working with a German Production Designer called Harry Lang, a man of great artistic talent and a BAFTA winner, but on this production, he seemed to be obsessed with chrome tape and 'Superglue'. I lost count of the number of times after a set had been dressed, you would find Harry with rolls of tape and glue 'titivating' bits of the set and sticking 'odds and sods' onto things as if in the realms of things, it would make the slightest bit of difference.

To him it obviously did. He was the one with the BAFTA, after all. You could often see him standing back and hear him purring in his broad German accent...grrrrrrrrrrrrrrrrrreat! That sound was frequently mimicked by the Prop Men.

I sometimes wonder if the film should have been called 'The Grrrrrrrrrrrrrreat Muppet Caper.' (I couldn't resist that.)

What I didn't know when I started this picture, and what George had obviously been aware of, was that the Henson Organisation had already planned to follow 'The Great Muppet Caper' with a much larger production at the same studio right after shooting finished using the same crew, but this was a different venture for them set in a mystical world of strange creatures and locations. It was to be called 'The Dark Crystal'.

This was to be a longer production than 'Muppet Caper' and would mean me being at Elstree Studios for nearly eighteen months, the longest continuous run of work I ever achieved in my career, but with that came the problem of being away from home so much with Ellenna growing quickly and me not seeing a great deal of that. Added to all that, Ann and I had decided to have another baby who was due around August/September time in 1981. This would be difficult because shooting on 'The Dark Crystal' would be going on until September, so I may need to pull out before the end to be there at the birth.

Any time I could get home became more important as Ann's pregnancy progressed, and the demands of looking after Ellenna and having a new baby on the way were going to be taxing, to say the least. I hated arriving late Friday nights after a long drive, having time with my family and having to get back in the car on Sunday night and drive away from them again.

From the outside, working in films looks very glamorous, but it does have its drawbacks, but you either go with it or get out. For the time being, the pros outweighed the cons, and we continued this path to a better life for us all.

So, after 'Muppet Caper' finished shooting, we continued straight on with 'Dark Crystal' without changing stride, but it was to be a much different film to work on for most of us.

CHAPTER II

THE DARK CRYSTAL

In a place outside time lies a mystical realm of sound and vision. A wondrous civilisation, where 'Good' and 'Evil' struggle to possess the 'Dark Crystal'. On another planet in the distant past, a 'Gelfing' embarks on a quest to find the missing shard of a magical crystal and to restore order to his world. He encounters weird creatures like the 'Mystics' and the 'Skeksis' and travels through lands of weird and wonderful plants and animals.

This is part of the opening narrative to the film that sends you into a mystical world where no human exists and was an idea that Jim Henson had, where he strived to take people back to the dark days of the Brothers Grimm and their tales, and was set in a fairyland of strange creatures and surroundings, all of which had to be made from scratch from wonderful drawings created in the Production Design Department, based on the vision of conceptual designer, Brian Froud.

From the outset, this was going to be a very difficult film to pull off, as at the time, it would have been the only live-action film in which no human character makes an appearance, so everything had to be designed from Brian's conceptual drawings. Even when Brian Froud presented Jim Henson with the drawings, there was confusion, as Brian had misunderstood what Jim had asked him to do. Jim was going to call his film 'The Dark Chrysalis', referring to creatures called Skeksis and their dominance over the world, but he liked the concept art and integrated the idea of the crystal into the storyline. Jim's ideas came largely after he and his daughter got caught at an airport in a snowstorm and roughed out drawings and ideas on hotel note paper which later formed the basis of the film.

There are many reasons why this project could have failed, but Jim pushed on, and with a large team of very creative people around him, he succeeded. The ideas from his and Brian's head found their way onto paper in the form of drawings, which then started to come to life through Model Makers, Construction workers and Prop Men, of which I was one.

Many of the props and scenery had to be large and bulky but also light enough in weight to be moved around from set to set, and this initially presented a problem to both the Prop and Construction Departments.

Most construction scenery was made from wood or scaffold frames covered in plaster for shaping and painting. This method made them extremely heavy and cumbersome, and so another solution had to be found.

Little did I know that my dabbling in Rattan furniture in the 1970s would be the solution to this, and I would be thrown into an area of props I hadn't experienced before.

Making everything meant weeks and weeks of manufacture before shooting could begin and was very labour-intensive, involving many prop men and model makers being employed and small 'factories' sprang up all around the studio making weapons, furniture, jewellery, weird plants, etc. It was in one of these factories that the thought of using Rattan occurred to me. I had only made small pieces, but the principle was the same, as the material was light, sturdy, very flexible and came in various sizes, so we tried a prototype and showed it to the Art Department.

They liked it and, because I was the only one who had actually done this before, I was put in charge of production, so all the pressure came my way. Some of the objects needed to be 8 to 10 metres in length, but after some early setbacks we finally got into a production line and started knocking them out to order. There is generally a solution to most problems; it's just a matter of persevering and thinking things through. Fortunately, my previous experience helped in some way.

Once a frame was finished, it was coated in latex so it could be painted any colour necessary, and then we set about in earnest getting sets dressed with these strange objects.

They were difficult to move around, and we had a great deal of help from Construction, who had the forklift trucks and low-load trailers to do the job, but we often had to wait for them as they too were very busy and normally that would not have been a problem, but one day it became one.

Dressing a large set on the lot at EMI studios, the Art Department felt they needed another large piece to finish it, so they called me at my 'factory' and asked me to get one up to them. I called Constuction, who had the lift and trailer but not a driver, so I could do it if I wanted to. As I was in charge, I felt bound to oblige, but I had never driven a forklift before, let alone with a trailer attached to it, but what choice did I have?

For those of you who have driven a forklift, you will know it is not straightforward, but after a few minutes of pulling the wrong levers and seeing bits go everywhere, I managed to get it pointing in the right direction. We loaded the object, in this case, a 'wind tunnel' plant, on the trailer, and off I went in what was now a 15-metre procession. It was all fine until I got to the corner of a studio building and had to make a right turn, which would not have been such a problem if someone had not left a metal 'skip' there, full of rubbish. I had decided how to turn, but the skip narrowed the gap, and I could see I was never going to make it. I had to reverse and go again, but I didn't know how to do this. It is quite an alien thing to do to reverse a trailer with a forklift, and I made a complete 'pig's ear' of it, finding myself now squashed against a wall with no way out. I began to feel very hot and bothered and prayed for someone to walk round the corner and get me out of this, but that was not going to happen. The Art Department must have been wondering what the hell I was doing, so I needed help and ran back to the Prop Room, leaving my stricken vehicle wedged against the building.

After 10 minutes of ridicule, I got my help, and we physically had to unload the trailer, bump the back round and reload for me to get on my way. I also had an escort of helpers with me all the way to the lot, should I make another mess of it.

Arriving triumphantly at the set, I pulled alongside the Art Director.

"Any problems? It seemed to take a while," he said.

"No, just making sure it got here safely," I lied.

"Great. Can you back it up over there, then?" He smiled.

Back it up? I could feel the colour draining from my face. Then everyone laughed, and the penny dropped. Word had preceded me of my disastrous journey, and I had to eat 'humble pie' for a while, but when the 'wind tunnel' was put in place, it did look the part. I remember thinking, *I made that*, but made a complete mess of getting it there. Honours even.

If you see extracts from the film and look past the main characters in the background, many of those objects and weird plants came from my idea of using rattan as a material. It is one of the few films I worked on that I had such an input into prop making, and I feel quite proud of that contribution which is forever immortalised in film.

The huge scale on which sets were being constructed, and the problems that caused really highlighted to me how good George was as a Prop Master; and why he had achieved such a status in the industry.

An Art Director, with the greatest of intentions, had given us 6 small boxes of lichens and mosses to dress a set of such huge magnitude that you wouldn't have known they were there. I asked George to come and see what he was asking us to do, knowing full well what he would say.

The next day, George had arranged truckloads of bushes, trees, plants and anything else he could think of to be delivered to the set, and we used all of it. He wasn't afraid to make decisions and use the budget he was given to do the job, and it was these qualities that made him stand out from other Prop Masters I worked with.

One particular Prop Master that was a complete contrast to George when it came to 'providing', was a man named Phil Hobbs.

Denis and I had been asked to standby on a cheap TV version of 'Oliver Twist' by the Art Director, directly against the wishes of Phil. It was not a film George wanted to do, so Denis and I did it to keep the money coming in, and probably wished we hadn't bothered. We were to find out how good George was.

CHAPTER 12

GEORGE VS. PHIL

From the beginning Phil was unhelpful and clearly held a grudge about being told who to use as his standbys. He wouldn't even give us a script to break down, and some of the first words he said to us were:

"Just turn up. You'll have everything you need."

We should have left right then, as it all went downhill from there onwards. To save money on his budget and get 'brownie points' from Production, he would have everybody on the dressing crew travel round in a small 7-seater van rather than use their own transport, which was fine with only one set to dress, but with more than one, was entirely useless. It got known on the main unit as the 'Sunshine Coach' as it looked like people on holiday rather than a dressing crew. George would not have been seen dead in it, but this was Phil to a tee.

Time and time again Denis and I were left high and dry by our leader, having to improvise with what we had just to get through, and it wasn't going unnoticed by the First assistant. With George, we would have had any alternative possible and in large amounts, but this lack of support from Phil was to come to a head with dramatic consequences on a night when we were shooting a riot scene in London.

This was an instantaneous riot, not planned, where the people of 'Oliver Twist' London charged through the streets, smashing property, picking up all sorts of 'weapons' to fight the authorities, and the production had employed a large group of extras to be the crowd. This, with their budget, was an expensive night that had to be done just once and properly.

As the hour approached, there was no sign of the 'Sunshine coach' and the props we would need. The First had asked us if we had everything and was not best pleased when we said we had nothing yet as Phil hadn't arrived. He went storming off to contact the production to find out what was happening, and we just waited.

The First came back saying Phil was stuck in traffic with all the Prop men and the props after dressing another set. There was the problem with just one mode of transport that I mentioned.

Denis and I decided we had to do something and were just about to get going when the 'coach' pulled into the car park where we were. Out came the distinctive figures of Phil and his chargehand dressing prop.

Phil wasn't a large man; he was smaller and rounder and had the appearance of an old sea captain, as he always wore an old cap at a jaunty angle. His sidekick, who I have forgotten the name of, was much taller with long hair and had two feet that were different in size by three grades. He had to have his footwear specially made. The two of them together were an image to behold. As they sauntered over, I asked the inevitable question.

"Have you got the props we need for the crowd?"

"They're in the back," he casually announced.

I threw the back of the vehicle open and saw just one small box. As I opened it, I audibly gasped at what I saw. Phil had given us 12 large pink and white 'twist' design candles to give to a rioting crowd back in London in the 1800s.

"You are joking, Phil? We can't give them these. What are you thinking?" I said, trying to control my anger.

"Just dirty them up a bit. They'll be fine." He was serious.

"We can't offer these up to the First. We'll get laughed off the set," Denis said.

"No, Den. We'll do just that and tell him Phil says they'll be fine. Phil can come with us. Can't you, Phil?" I said, half dragging Phil towards the First, who was now on his way over to us. As he arrived, he could see the candles in my hand. He was as gobsmacked as we were.

"You are not handing those out. Where're all the other bits we need, Phil?" He was about an inch away from Phil's face.

At last, Phil seemed to be getting the message, but the First wasn't finished with him and laid into him in a big way, mentioning all the times he had hung Denis and me out to dry, etc., etc., and if things didn't improve his days were numbered.

Den and I looked at each other. We didn't have to say anything as we knew we had been stuffed again. While Phil was getting lambasted by the First, we went about our business of creating 'riot props' from nothing. We had some old-bought furniture we smashed up, took pieces of wood and wrapped them in old sacking for torches, and so on until we had enough to offer up and make it look like a rioting crowd.

As always, it got done, and we got the shots, but the whole episode showed the effects different actions can cause. George would never have been in that situation. He would have worked out weeks ago what was needed, and it all would have been there.

Phil did it on a wing and a prayer and hoped it would get through unnoticed. If you were to put 'Dark Crystal' and 'Oliver Twist' together, Phil would have been the man giving us 6 small crates of lichen to dress a set the size of a superstore. George would be the one with 4 truckloads sitting outside the stage, should you need it.

George had tried all his career to enhance the reputation of Prop Men and to get them more recognised for their input. That thought hadn't even crossed Phil's mind. If he could ride around in his vehicle and get things done as cheaply as possible, he would be happy.

That's why, for example, if you Google 'George Ball, Property Master', you'll see the list of 49 credits from 1961 to 2002, and some of the films like Superman, The Omen, etc., he was Prop Master on. (I couldn't find Phil.)

Even I can be found, but they have given me three more credits that were someone else's, but at least I made the scratch.

The image of Phil and his sidekick getting out of a battered old 7-seater coach stuck in my mind. Was that really how we wanted to be seen as representative of Prop Men, or was George's approach a better way forward?

There was no doubt in my mind. I spent the rest of my career working with George, and he was never called out in front of the unit like Phil was. I never worked with Phil again, but there was a rumour that the old 'sunshine coach' had been sighted moving around London, so he must have been still getting work.

It sounds like a shallow concept talking about creating an 'image', but I realised that pretty much everyone does just that, whether they realise they are doing it or not. For example, no one wants to be hated, so they take steps to avoid that happening if they can. Everything you do is a calculation of the effect it has on other people and comes down to basics. We all wanted to be liked and thought of as good at our jobs so we would simply get more work. Our 'Image' was vital in an industry where 'Image' was what we strived to achieve.

As we neared the end of 'Dark Crystal', the decision to leave early because of our second daughter, Ria, being born was looming. We had a rough date, and I certainly was not going to put myself in the same position as I was when Ellenna was born, so I had a talk with George, and we decided that I should go home with plenty of time to spare this time.

We had planned a home birth for Ria, but at the last minute there was a complication, and we had to go into hospital. It was all fine in the end, but it once again highlighted the problems of being away from home so much. We had to address this situation, as it was no good for any of us.

CHAPTER 13

THE MOVE

It was now 1982. I had surpassed the 'work for two years and decide then' theory I had formulated with Les back in 1978, and it was becoming obvious that my career was going to continue in films. We had financially steadied ourselves, but our family life was a shambles that needed sorting out, and after a lot of discussion Ann and I decided that, while the girls were still young enough that moving schools wouldn't matter, it would be better for us all if we moved nearer to where I would, generally, be working. I wouldn't be away so much; I could see Ann and see the girls growing up and maybe have a social life.

After doing some research, we settled on trying to find a house in Surrey, just outside London, but with good links to the main studios. It wasn't the cheapest of areas, but its location was really important, so we started looking.

The number of houses that we got details for that we couldn't afford was horrendous, and the ones we could afford were so far away from where we wanted to be it wasn't worth going to see them. We were beginning to wonder if this was a good idea after all, as it just didn't seem to be working for us. The theory of moving closer to where I normally worked was sound, and it would have drastically improved our lives, but making it happen was turning into a nightmare. We called every estate agent we could find in the relevant area, but no one had anything remotely suitable, and as a last resort Ann and I decided we would drive up again for one last look at where we needed to be and reassure ourselves this was right for us.

We hadn't anything to see as we motored up the roads and motorways that had become very familiar to me over the last few years, and both of us were quiet on the way up, thinking our plans may need to be rethought. As we drove into a small town called Cobham, where some of the estate agents we were dealing with had their offices, we couldn't find a parking space anywhere. This was going so well. Up and down we went, and in pure frustration I turned off the main high street into a side road I had never been down before. Slowly we edged our way down this street, looking for somewhere to park and, finally, there was a space we pulled into and right where we parked was a small estate agent's office which we hadn't even heard of.

As we got out of the car, we read each other's minds and decided to give it a look, so in we went. There was a man sitting at a desk on the phone to a client and, on seeing us enter, beckoned for us to sit down.

It was a tiny office, so it was impossible not to hear what was being said on the phone, and the more we listened, the more interested we became. He was obviously taking on a new house and getting a few details, and what he was describing seemed to fit the bill for us. We couldn't wait for him to finish his conversation and put the receiver down so we could tackle him. Finally, he stopped talking and put the phone down.

"Sorry about that. What can I do for you?" he asked.

"I think you already have done it. The house you were discussing sounds exactly what we are after. Can we go and see it?" I said.

He was more surprised than us and explained he hadn't seen it himself, so there wasn't an exact price, but he gave us a rough idea. Amazingly, it was in our price range. We were very excited. Could this finally be the answer to our dreams?

He picked the phone up and called the owner back, not more than 5 minutes after the previous call. To be told she had a viewing so quickly must have totally taken her by surprise, but she was delighted to oblige and, twenty minutes later, we were standing outside what we hoped would be our new home.

It was lovely, in a quiet cul-de-sac, overlooking a large park and the right size for our growing family. The lady was so nice and inviting and showed us round, told us how great the neighbourhood was, about local schools, supermarkets, etc. As we got back in our car, we were hooked and already making plans for the house without having agreed a price yet. Do we drive home and think about it or make the decision now while we were there and the first to see it? Within 10 minutes we were in the estate agent's office again, discussing our offer. He called the lady while we were there, and after a small discussion he smiled and nodded at us. Our offer had been accepted, and she would take her house off the market.

On the way back we spoke a lot about our new house, what we could do to it, what it could do for us and how our lives would be so different now I no longer had to do such tiring journeys in the car and be away from home so much.

This was our fairy tale come true, and we couldn't wait for it to begin. It all seemed to be slotting into place as we sold our house very quickly and were in our new place in a few months.

We had a lot on our plate at this time. Ria was barely 6 or 7 months old, Ellenna was about 3 and a half years old, we had moved across the country to a new house which we had to do some work on, and I had been taking on bits of work to keep the money rolling in to pay for the move and the alterations we wanted to make, before starting another film with George in March of that year.

After 4 years on the road, coming home every night was going to feel strange for a while, and I had gotten used to being around in our new house when George phoned and said he had a date for starting on the next film. It was a bittersweet moment knowing I had to start back on full-time work, but I had just received a call from one of the best Prop Masters in the country talking about our next film. OUR next film!

I didn't know anything about it other than the name 'The Missionary', but it was to bring home to me that the film industry is not there to accommodate you, rather the reverse, and no matter where you lived, it would never make it easy for you.

CHAPTER 14

THE MISSIONARY

In 1906, the Reverend Charles Fortesque is recalled from his work in Africa. He sits having tea in an establishment with his Bishop, who asks him how he is with women. Charles is taken aback. He doesn't understand the question. The bishop goes on to explain.

"I know you're good at everything else, but how are you with women? I want you to find out why they do what they do and stop them doing it."

He is referring to 'Women of the night', not something Charles is familiar with, nor wants to be, but this is a direct order from his Bishop that he must obey, and so the scene is set for this very funny film to unfold.

Our plans to move closer appeared to be spot on as the main studio for this film was Shepperton, just 20 minutes down the road and, in the first few weeks of setting up, it was absolute bliss from my point of view. Not too early a start, and home every night and weekend. Just what we had ordered, but the 'Missionary' also had locations, one of which was in Scotland for several weeks. I had to accept that or turn down a great career with a Prop Master who could pick and choose his work and make my family's lives so much better. You remember me mentioning that if you got in with a Prop Master, you had to do the films he wanted to do. This was such an occasion, so Ann and I resolved to go along with this, and I stuck with the film.

As it turns out, it was one of the nicest films I ever worked on. The crew were great; the cast was great, the Scottish location was beautiful, and everyone got on so well. What more could you ask for, other than being able to move Scotland closer to Surrey?

The production company was called 'HandMade Films', and one of the Producers was none other than George Harrison. Yes, the Beatle George Harrison!

Richard Loncraine was directing it after making his name in commercials and inventing some executive toys. (Not sure if that is relevant, but a fact nevertheless.) Everywhere he went, he took his huge 'Winnebago' mobile home with him.

It had a cast list to die for, including Michael Palin, Maggie Smith, Trevor Howard, Denholm Elliott, Michael Hordern, David Suchet, Phoebe Nicholls, and Timothy Spall. Some of the funniest actors around at the time, and during takes they were so good you had to prevent yourself from laughing out loud.

It was a fast-moving film with many locations, a lot of them around parts of the East End of London, and it was a fair old job for the Dressing crew keeping up with all the sets.

Set back in 1906, many of the locations were picked to reflect the period, but others were adapted to make it look that way. On a bombed-out section of London near the Columbia Road flower market, the construction had built a façade of terraced houses to create a 1906 street.

Richard Loncraine tells the story that one day, while he was there, an old lady was standing glancing at the houses and seemed extremely sad and upset. He went over to see if he could comfort her and asked why she was crying.

"My house came back!" she said.

She was convinced in her mind that one of the houses in the street was the one she was born in. Maybe the photo of the street that the construction worked from just happened to be the road she lived on. Who knows? But it does show the memories that filmmaking can evoke in people.

Once the locations around London were finished, we were off to Scotland to a beautiful house by the side of Ardverikie Loch in the Scottish Highlands. The weather was fabulous, which is exactly what we needed to shoot in, and it made working out in the open so pleasant. These were good times.

As the location was so remote, there were no large hotels nearby to accommodate the film crew, so we were all based in a hotel about an hour away from the house, which provided logistical problems for everyone and their equipment getting there.

The Production Manager, Graham Ford, in an effort to save on transport costs, decided in his infinite wisdom not to have transport for each department, but instead to put everyone in a large coach and leave and arrive together. Great idea on paper, but if you have any idea of how films are made, then totally impracticable. Each department has a role to fill, and that often entails arriving earlier than others or staying later. You can probably see where I am going with this.

The journey by coach was longer than by car, obviously, and some of the roads to gain access to the house involved someone physically getting out of the coach and opening and shutting a gate behind them.

On the first day, we all tried to get on this one coach with all sorts of equipment. It was chaos. To be at the location by 8.30am when we were supposed to start shooting, we really needed to have left the hotel by 7.30am at the latest. The time everyone was rounded up and aboard the 'Ardverikie Express', it was around 8am. Graham was doing his nut, and the Producers were not very happy either, but off we set. We were beset by sheep on the roads and all manner of delays, and it was gone 9am when we finally arrived.

No one had eaten breakfast yet, and no department had had a chance to get set up to shoot. This was becoming a farce of epidemic proportions, and Richard, who had stayed at the house in his Winnebago and avoided all this nonsense, was livid.

One benefit of shooting in such locations is the beautiful light you get, particularly early mornings and evening dusks, and Richard was now losing the morning light because of the transport arrangements. That would affect how we could shoot for the rest of the day and for continuity in filming.

Eventually, we were ready, and we soldiered on as best we could through the rest of the day, but we all still had to get back to the hotel, and we only had the coach to do it in.

At the end of the day, Graham was like a mother hen trying to get everyone back on the coach, but each department takes a different amount of time to pack up, so until the very last person was on the coach, we couldn't leave. It was 8pm before the coach pulled out of the drive and just after 9pm when we got back to the hotel. The problem for Graham was that after 5.30pm everyone was on overtime rate, so most of the crew had to be paid an extra 3 and half hours overtime. Ouch! This had been a production disaster and a very expensive one.

As we sat down to our late supper, memos came out from the production that the coach for tomorrow had been cancelled, and from here on individual departments would now have their own transport available. What a surprise!

In the morning, outside the hotel, there was a string of Ford Escorts with our department names on them, and we were to take our own lead as to what times we would leave the hotel to fulfil our tasks so that the camera would turn over by 8.30am.

I think Graham may have had a little ear bashing from Production over his cost-cutting idea.

Things did improve greatly from then on, and each day you could see a fleet of Escorts flying up and down the Highland roads. I suppose with a name like Graham Ford, Escorts would be an obvious choice. It did seem a very popular car locally, and there were many to be seen en route.

One day as we were passing through a small town that had cars parked on both sides of the road, making it difficult to get through, I noticed another Escort coming into town from the opposite direction to us. We had both made our decisions to carry on, but as we neared each other, we began to doubt ourselves. This was going to be tight, and within seconds the cars were on each other. There was a dull thud as we passed, and we both stopped to see what had happened.

Looking out of my window, I could see the driver's wing mirror hanging off, and the same had happened to the other driver. With identical cars, the mirrors had been at exactly the same height and had hit each other. We were both at fault, so no point in going through insurance procedures. We had a laugh at the stupidity of it, shook hands and off we went again, with our mirror now being held up by gaffer tape as any self-respecting Prop Man would do.

Eventually, we arrived at the location, and there was no time to sort this out now, but I was wondering what Graham might have to say. The glass was broken, but I managed to get the unit back in its mountings, so I thought if I could replace the mirror, I wouldn't have to tell him at all.

There was a handyman who worked at the house, so I asked him if he had a spare bit I could use. Not only did he have some, but he also offered to cut the piece for me if I gave him the measurements. Result! I told him it was a secret from production so to go through me, and he gave me a wink to say he understood.

At the end of the day, he approached me with all the finesse of an amateur spy and handed me a cloth-covered bundle.

"That should do the trick," he said, winking.

I was busy, so put it to one side until the end of the day. When I had time, I removed the cloth to reveal the thickest lump of mirror I had seen, and nibbled round the edges with a pair of pliers to make the shape. It was awful and totally unusable, but I couldn't tell him that after all the trouble he had gone through. So much for my plan, and I had handed him a bit of money for his work as well.

Nothing else to do now but come clean and tell Graham, which is what I should have done in the first place. Prop Man's ego. Think you can fix anything.

Graham was fine with it. He actually laughed about the incident, and it got fixed. The next day the odd job man sauntered up and asked me if it had fitted ok.

"Yes, perfect. Thanks for all your help," I lied.

"Well, if you want anything else done, just ask," he replied.

I smiled. Probably not likely.

Unfortunately, this was not the end of the misfortunes for our old Escort, for while at the house, we had to go up into the hills around the area to film a pheasant shoot and to include the panoramic views available; we climbed up high where the access was rugged and challenging.

Production had hired some all-terrain vehicles, but not enough for everyone, and we weren't considered important enough, so our only mode of transport to the peak was our Escort, a vehicle hardly appropriate to use in these conditions.

As Standbys, we had to take a lot of our equipment with us, as well as the props we needed, so we loaded up and went for it. Initially we were going well, but as we climbed, the ruts got deeper, and we could hear the bottom of the car scraping on the earth. If you stopped, you would not get going again, so we prayed and pushed on until there was an almighty thud under the car, all sorts of indicator lights flashed on the dashboard, and we came to a grinding halt.

As we got out to inspect the damage, we could see lots of oil spilling out onto the hilly track and realised we had ripped the sump cover off the bottom of the engine. The Unit was still some distance away, so we couldn't carry everything, and our only solution was to wait for help as in those days, mobile phones were not in common use, so we couldn't call anyone.

As luck would have it, one of the location managers was coming up the hill in a proper vehicle and, after the usual piss take, took us and our cargo up the mountain to the unit, leaving the Escort stuck in the way of everyone going up and down.

I didn't think the odd job man would be able to help with this one, so I had to tell Graham, who was not best pleased although it was partly his fault we were in this situation, but give him his due, he did have a replacement back at the house when we got down from the hills, with a note attached saying.

"Don't break this one."

Fortunately, we did look after that one.

Our stay in Scotland was coming to an end, and to show his appreciation to the crew, Richard wanted to throw a party by the Loch at the house, so preparations were made to make this happen.

Richard had a party trick he liked to perform and approached us to see if we had any Gun Cotton he could use. This is a substance that, when lit, burns like a bomb fuse. Relatively safe if you know what you are doing with it, but we didn't have any, only another more potent substance that contains magnesium and burns a lot hotter. You need some knowledge when handling this.

We had no idea what his 'Act' was, and he was insistent on having something, so he took some with our cautionary advice, but he was the boss.

On the night of the party, we had great weather and sitting next to the Loch was idyllic. Music played, drinks were downed, and the whole atmosphere was so relaxing, knowing there were coaches waiting to take us home. There was even flirting going on, and many rumours circulated after that night.

Not about me, I hasten to add.

Around 9pm, Richard took the stage wearing a bowler hat with a light bulb on the top, which was attached to a battery, making it glow. He was also carrying a pair of silver spoons, which he proceeded to play on his limbs whilst accompanied by a man on a guitar. Yes, I know. Bizarre!

As the music rose to a crescendo, Richard took a lighter from his pocket, lit it, and attempted to put the flame to the rim of his hat. It took a number of attempts before he finally achieved the required result. There was an almighty flash, and a great mushroom cloud of smoke appeared above his head. Quite spectacular in effect, but what not many people had noticed, while distracted by the spectacular, was the substance we had given him had burned so hot it had scorched all of his hand and wrist where he held the lighter. He dropped the spoons and ran to the Loch to dowse his hand in the cold water.

This was clearly not the way this was supposed to end, and we had to call an ambulance, which took a while due to the remoteness of the location, but in the interim, he was tended to by the unit nurse.

He had done a lot of damage and appeared the next day sporting a huge 'bulb' shaped bandage on his hand, which was ironic considering the design of his hat.

He must have been in a lot of pain for the rest of the film, but he saw it through to the end and produced a really funny film that I think got its money back, which was great for a little company like HandMade, who gave a lot of untried people a chance to prove themselves. Vital to maintaining film production.

I loved working on this film and got to work with some of the cast later on in my career, particularly Michael Palin, but in all the time I worked on films, I worked with the same Director only twice, Jim Henson, because he did one film straight after another and Dick Clement for HandMade. I suppose their commitment to a film runs over a much longer time than most of the crew, so the number of projects they do are likely to be less, but most of the Directors I worked with I liked, and they all had their own ways of doing things which you will see later in the book.

Now it was time to get back to my family and have a rest before the dreaded 'Oliver Twist' started, and it was so nice to be home again, although, as things turned out, it would not be our home for as long as I thought it would.

While I was away, Ann still had to have a life, and she had really made a lot of friends around the area, helped by the common factor of young children going to nursery school, where she met other mums with kids of the same age. This is something that I was never a part of, and my circle of friends, who were mostly in the film industry, by comparison, was small. I needed to be at home more often to change this, but I couldn't pick my films to suit me or dictate where I wanted them to be shot, so this was a problem that was only going to get worse, and the next film after 'Oliver' was to add to this, and also highlight what I was saying about different Directors' approaches.

A few days after finishing on the 'Missionary', the phone rang at home. The call was from a company that had got my name from someone and was offering me a job, not on a film but on a commercial. I hadn't done one since the disastrous French Shoe commercial and wasn't overly keen to do another one, but it was a week's work at a very good rate of pay, and at that point I didn't have any work lined up. I had made that mistake in the past about turning work down if you remember, and I wasn't going to do that again. Besides, I was much more experienced now and more confident in what I was doing, so after discussing it with Ann, I agreed to do it.

CHAPTER 15

THE COMMERCIAL

I had never worked for this particular company before, which was not surprising, so I did not know what to expect. It was for a 'Ford Transit Van' commercial starting off at a studio in Battersea in London and then moving on to Scotland. (Why always Scotland?)

The first morning, I turned up at the 'Studio' bright and early. It wasn't so much a studio but more a converted church in the middle of a row of terraced houses. Quentin Masters was the Director and also owned the studio, as well as some of the terraced houses on either side of the church to house some of his full-time crew.

Quentin was a lovable rogue who liked to earn money, so he had set all of this up and wore so many hats in order to extract as much of the client's money as he could for himself. The terraced houses were for young men, mostly from Australia, who had come to England for an adventure and to earn a bit of money. Quentin provided both of these in exchange for their help on his films. He paid well below the going rate for normal crew, but charged the client the full whack, pocketing the difference.

I arrived to find the studio locked up, which was frustrating as I always liked to be in early so I could set all my equipment up, so I rang the bell. Getting no answer, I decided to walk around the church, sorry Studio, to see if there was another entrance, but there wasn't, and there was no sign of life anywhere. Then a lady walking by with her dog, seeing my confusion, shouted over saying to try one of the terraced houses as they were probably all still asleep. (She was obviously a local.)

I thanked her and walked off in the direction of the first house, which wasn't locked but had a bent nail on the outside to stop the door from swinging in. On the outside? Couldn't get my head around that.

I knocked, but there was no reply, and after a second attempt I decided to bend the nail back and go in. It was really dark inside, so I called out and from the blackness came a weary voice, and a figure loomed out of the gloom.

"I'm trying to get in the studio, but it's locked. Does anyone have the key?" I asked.

In a broad Australian accent, he told me that Greg would have it.

"And where is he?" I went on.

"He's in the back room somewhere," he replied and wandered back into his lair.

As I edged my way down the hallway, I noticed another body curled up in a sleeping bag under the stairs. No mattress or pillow, just the bag. Reaching the backroom, I could vaguely make out at least another 4 inhabitants. My God, how many were in this house? I hadn't been upstairs yet!

At the door, I shouted out Greg's name. One of the four bodies stirred in the darkness, and a tired voice, once again Australian, acknowledged me.

"I need the key to the studio. Do you have it?"

"What time is it, mate?" he said.

"About twenty to eight," I replied.

"Shit, I've overslept. Be right with you," he said, struggling to get his trousers on.

Five minutes later, he was at the studio door with the key. I guessed he was skipping the shower and teeth cleaning that morning.

There was a slow flow of half-asleep, dishevelled Aussie crew now turning up at the studio looking for breakfast. Word had clearly gotten round that it was time for work. They would probably leave the making of beds and vacuuming until later, I thought.

The studio was tiny, and the Transit van took up a fair amount of space, but they planned to make it look like the van was moving. I have to admit to having my doubts about this, but this was Quentin's way of saving money, so with wind machines and a powder called 'Fullers Earth', we set about creating this illusion. Within minutes of starting, we could not see more than a metre in front of us with all the dust, and no one had masks or breathing gear, so we were inhaling this stuff. It was quite ridiculous. There were frequent 'air breaks' taken by everyone, but this went on all day until Quentin was satisfied. I don't think any of his crew had the courage to complain for fear of being 'Aus-tracised'. (Sorry!).

I went home with a really sore throat and pounding headache, which was compounded by the fact that we were driving up to Scotland the next day.

It wasn't to improve much up there, as Quentin had his own way of doing things and was a forceful enough character to run roughshod over anyone complaining. Trying to put too much in one day, we were racing all over the place from one location to another, but it wasn't possible to do all of it, so we got behind.

A second unit was formed, which I was on, to do a shot of the Transit racing along a mountain road and swerving around a fallen tree to show the van's manoeuvrability, but unfortunately, the professional driver was with the main unit, so Quentin was looking for a volunteer, which was obviously going to be me.

He asked me as if I had a choice in the matter, and the next minute I was sitting in the driver's seat getting instructions. I knew Quentin wouldn't have covered this scenario with insurance, so I wasn't going to perform any heroics here.

The First called 'Action', and I hit the accelerator and shot off down the track at a rate of knots towards the tree. As I approached, I noticed the road fell away dramatically at the edges, leaving little room to manoeuvre. I hit the brakes, swung the wheel to the left, then to the right, and somehow got round the tree, but it didn't feel as if the back wheels were supported by much, so I slammed the brakes on and skidded to a halt. That's me done, I thought; I'm not doing that again.

As I got out and went to inspect the van, I saw the left rear wheel wasn't actually touching the ground, and the van was resting on just three wheels overhanging a severe drop. A four-letter word beginning with 's' and ending with 't' left my lips.

By this time, everyone had arrived at the van.

"Are you alright?" Quentin said.

"Not really. You might need someone else if you are going to do that again," I said.

"No, you did well. We can use that," Quentin replied.

The old 'wing and a prayer' Quentin strategy had triumphed again, and as it was the last shot of the day, the unit moved on to our accommodation at a harbour town called Ullapool, which was pretty but only had one hotel and a number of small pubs. As in films, the elite were in the hotel and the plebs in the pubs. (I'll leave you to guess where I was.)

In our pub, there was only one bathroom and 9 of us, all wet, tired, hungry and wanting a bath or a shower. It would have taken us all night with one bathroom, by which time all the restaurants would be shut, so there was definite unrest in the camp, which was turning into hostility. After a small discussion, we decided to take this further, so armed with our towels and shampoo, we headed off to the hotel to air our grievances.

As we entered the hotel restaurant, we saw the elite all nicely washed and sitting and eating their gourmet meals. The sight of us certainly turned a few heads, and Quentin rose from his table to confront us.

"What's up, lads?" he enquired.

After a brief run-down of our complaints, he asked us what we wanted him to do about it.

"We want keys from enough rooms so we can all have a proper wash," said the Gaffer Spark (chief electrician), who, by the way, was a huge man and probably not one you would want to cross.

"We can't do that; these are people's rooms." Quentin protested.

"Well, it's either that or none of us will be working tomorrow," said the Gaffer.

Soon there was an array of bedroom keys before us, and we all selected one and headed off to get washed.

There was a strange atmosphere on the unit the following morning, with a lot of resentment about the way the crew was being treated, and there was definitely a whiff of revenge in the air as we set up on a large jetty looking out to sea.

At the end of the jetty there was a small building housing a toilet, and before shooting began Quentin had decided to use its facilities and disappeared inside. Not sure where this idea came from, but I had a small wooden wedge in my pocket for emergencies, which I pushed under the bottom of the half-glazed door, preventing it from opening outwards and then moved away, pretending to do my job.

Quentin appeared and tried to push the door, which wouldn't move. He pushed harder, but the wedge was doing its job, so he pushed at it with his shoulder. It held fast, and you could see his frustration was mounting, so he started banging loudly on the door to get attention. We all feigned surprise and 'rushed' to help.

"Are you alright, Quentin?" I shouted through the glass.

"No, can't get the bloody door open," he screamed.

"What have you done to it? It was fine when I went in there," I enquired.

"I haven't done anything. Can you get me out?"

I feigned pulling from my side, and told him to bang the top corner with his fist, which he obligingly did. I knew nothing would change, so I told him to kick the bottom corner. He was going at it with increasing anger, but the wedge stopped any movement, so we told him to do both movements at once.

The sight of our director banging, kicking, and screaming was a picture. Finally, I thought we had exhausted this, so I told him to stop.

"Oh, I think I know what it is. Someone has put a small wedge under the door. Have you upset anyone lately?" I said.

We were all laughing as we let him out of his make-piece prison.

"You bastards," he bellowed. "Very bloody funny."

He actually took it very well and saw the funny side of it, but I did notice he was a bit wary from then on about how he treated us. Maybe a lesson learned, but I doubt that with Quentin.

I thought he might have had the last laugh and make us all wait for our invoices to be paid, but it didn't happen, and we all got paid quickly. Maybe he thought I might come back with my wedge.

Our paths never crossed again, so he might have had the last laugh, but fortunately the industry was quite busy, and so with this commercial and one or two other bits on films, I scrambled through until George found a new picture for us all. I say 'us all' for we had become a little group that was now moving together from film to film. I felt more secure in that thought than when I first ventured on to a set with Les back in the day.

Now it was off to Shepperton again, which was always good for me just living 20 minutes away.

CHAPTER 16

THE KEEP

As the camera draws back, we see a long contingent of Second World War German military vehicles as they make their way through a drab Romanian village toward an imposing medieval stone built 'Keep'. A high-ranking German officer dismounts from the lead vehicle to survey their new home as the villagers look on in fear. These are their new masters, and they have no say in the matter.

One of the scenes from this film that quite easily might never have been made and consequently never have appeared in this book, but it had a point to make and forced itself onto celluloid.

It had been budgeted at the time to be made for $10.75 million, but they could only raise $10.2 million, so there had to be a page-ripping exercise to trim it down.

While this was going on, none of us were working, and to hedge his bets, George got himself involved with another film called 'Gossip' in case 'The Keep' didn't get made. (See, a man with choices.)

Either way, we would have a film to work on, and in the

end, it was 'Gossip' that ran into problems and, to my knowledge, never made the can, but 'The Keep' raised the required finances provided it finished principal shooting by Christmas 1982. Principal meant all main unit shooting, not special effects, etc. I tell you this fact, for you will see how silly a statement this is by the end of the film.

Michael Mann was the Director who had made his name on a very successful American TV series called 'Miami Vice'. So, we had a 'Mann' for the job, so to speak. (Sorry! Again.)

He had a reputation for not tolerating failure in any form that it manifested itself, and a few people on this film were to find this out very quickly. He knew exactly what he wanted, and nothing and nobody was going to change that, so that set the scene for one hell of a production.

Denis and I read our scripts to acquaint ourselves with the problems ahead, and after we both looked at each other. Our thoughts were the same, the script was awful, and we wondered why anyone would put up the money to make this. It had some good actors as well who obviously hadn't read it before signing on the dotted line. My only thoughts were that Michael was such a name at that moment and was so passionate about making this into his vision that everyone went along with it. He was such a forceful man, and no one liked to say no to him.

The Romanian Keep held the 'Evil' half of a monster within its walls, which were encrusted with gold crosses. The German guards noticed the crosses and their potential value and started prising them out with their bayonets, and this began to release the evil from the Keep, which started devouring the soldiers and taking on human form. The 'Good' side is then summoned from his nice little house in the Mediterranean to fight the 'Evil'. That's it, pretty much.

As the 'Evil' evolves, it takes on various guises, and to gauge the progress, each stage was shown to the crew for their reaction. The first stage looked like a Grand Prix racing driver had

had his suit shredded by a 'Stanley' knife, and the crew had to do their best not to laugh; it was so bad. We should have realised at this point what was to follow and run for the hills, but we didn't to our everlasting cost.

We had a strict schedule to get it done, but Michael was such a perfectionist. Each shot took forever, and within a short space of time we were behind. Every day we dropped shots to be made up later, and the list was mounting to the point where Production asked us if we could work some overtime to catch up.

I should explain at this stage that you had to be in a Union to work on films, and each film had a 'Union Representative' appointed out of the crew to make sure the crew was being treated correctly.

I don't know how this happened, but it was me that was chosen, and having never done this before, I didn't know what to expect. After this film, it was something I would not be doing again, I can tell you.

It started fine. We agreed on a couple more hours a night, and everyone was happy, except Michael, who quite clearly would have liked to go on all night and expected everyone to feel the same. We didn't!

Two weeks later, I was back in the Producers office negotiating more terms and conditions to work more overtime as Michael wanted to work until 10pm every night, and those who would not oblige were told to go home at 5.30pm to be replaced by a substitute, as if this were a football match. This wouldn't work, but he would not be told, and also working until 10pm each night evoked a union ruling that on the fifth day, the crew could not come in until 2pm to start shooting. 'Red rag to a bull' comes to mind.

Now I was stuck in the middle of an argument I didn't want, trying to appease the crew and Michael, but as was the way Michael won, and we started working longer hours with part-timers coming in for the evening. I'd never seen this and wondered if it had ever happened before. This was a very costly exercise for Production on a very tight budget, but hopefully, we would be able to pull back on the shots we had lost and get back on schedule.

No such luck. A week later I was back in the office again, being asked if we could work until 11pm each night, but the crew had had enough and said no, so Colin, the Producer, agreed to appoint a Production Manager to monitor the situation and stop Michael at the agreed time of 10pm. Right!

A few days later, a very tall, officious-looking Production Manager called Patrick arrived on set with the obligatory clipboard under his arm. As the bewitching hour approached, all eyes were on Patrick, wondering how he would deal with this. His eyes were fixed on his watch as the seconds ticked on, and then he made his move. Across the stage he strode to where Michael was standing and confronted him full-on with the facts. There was a brief conversation, after which Patrick turned on his heels and disappeared off stage. We think he may have been put in his place, for the rest of us carried on shooting until Michael was satisfied.

We didn't see much of Patrick after that, and kept on shooting until late every night. Colin obviously could not control Michael and had to contend with the fact that the overtime was costing the Production a lot of money. We were all tired, and the only consolation was that we were earning a fortune, but none of us were seeing our families very much, and we still had two location shoots to do, which would mean being away from home all the time.

One of these locations was in a small fishing village in Portugal. It was here that we were to shoot the 'Good' side arriving by boat from his Stucco village destination, so the Art Department was sent out earlier than the unit to pick out a suitable fishing trawler that Michael would like the hero to arrive on.

They displayed an array of 14 assorted boats for him to look at, and during the small amount of time we weren't shooting, he flew out to view them. Slowly he walked past them all as if inspecting the guard, and at the end of the line he stopped. He didn't like any of them! However, he had spotted another boat he did like, and the Art Department had to try to explain to him that this was, in fact, a sand dredger and would our 'Hero' be arriving on a sand dredger?

Michael was unmoved by the argument and insisted that if we cut bits off it and added some other bits, it would work. The cost and time delay in doing this was pointed out, and eventually he was persuaded to go with one of the 14, although he never really liked it.

The 'Hero' stands thoughtfully at the front of the boat, contemplating his future actions as we shoot this against the backdrop of a white Stucco village lit up in the night sky. This was the theory; now we had to put this into practice.

The location for the boat was selected so we could see the village behind us, and the electricians had brought huge lamps which burnt carbon sticks to give the light intensity needed to light the backdrop, but the sticks burnt out quickly and had to be constantly monitored and replaced. They were also very expensive and needed an army of 'Sparks' to service this appetite, so from 6pm onwards, they went about their duties.

Meanwhile, a small shooting unit, including myself, boarded the 'chosen' vessel and set out to sea. I was not good on the high seas, so I wasn't looking forward to this.

The boat was quite basic, with a small, covered area for the Skipper and a few crew members and a lot of deck for dealing with the catch. Not much else to see and nowhere to go if it rained, or we had to get out of shot.

We started shooting, not looking once at the lit hillside village but purely out to sea in the now fading light. Michael wanted to see, and I kid you not, highlighted seagulls in the air at night. The Lighting Cameraman was suitably unimpressed but did his best to oblige by using small 'Sun-Gun' lights to pick them out, with seriously not a lot of success.

After a while, we forgot this nonsense and embarked on more serious shooting with the actor Scott Glenn. To make the shot wider, the camera was set at the back end of the boat, with the 'Hero' at the front, leaving very little room to hide the crew and equipment. It meant some of the crew literally lying on their backs on the deck as low as possible out of camera shot, and this was on a rolling fishing trawler at night in the middle of the Ocean. Not for the faint-hearted if you are prone to seasickness, but with the weird things that were happening on this film, it seemed like a normal request.

As the darkness devoured the boat, we never once looked back to the lit village, which was costing an arm and a leg to achieve. Remember the budget? Then, out of the darkness, some lights appeared. It turned out to be another fishing vessel on its way back to harbour and was known to our skipper, so they briefly drew alongside each other. Michael's eyes lit up.

This was the fishing boat he had envisaged and now wanted. There were some quick discussions in Portuguese, some money changed hands, and before we knew it, the whole crew with their equipment was clambering off one fishing vessel in complete darkness, in the middle of the Ocean, onto another to start shooting again. My Union Rules didn't cover this situation, so I said nothing.

As midnight approached, a message came over the radio from the Producer asking if we still needed the village lit up, the one, remember, that we had never looked at. He was worried about the mounting cost and wanted to stop paying the 'Sparks' after midnight when it turned into serious money. By the time the answer got back to shore and relayed to the Electricians, it was debatable, depending on whose watch you went by if the stop order was before or after the bewitching hour. This argument went on for weeks before a compromise deal was made. Even more waste of money.

After that fiasco, we continued the following night doing

the close-ups and tighter shots in the Skipper's cabin, but this time in the harbour, with no less bizarre results.

Michael wanted to go off script and get some ad-lib acting from the actors by firing odd questions at them and getting their reactions. This line of filming seemed to go on forever, and the questions were quite ridiculous. One was, "What would you do if I kicked you in the leg?"

The answer given was, "I'd hop on the other one."

I don't believe any of this ended up in the film, and when we were so far behind with the main shooting, why did we waste time doing this? After a while, it became too much for the Production Designer, John Box, who stood up and walked off, muttering, "I'm not going to be associated with this shit."

He did have a lot of support with this, but we did what we usually did and carried on with this drivel until Michael decided to stop.

Back home in England, I was summoned to the Producer's office again to discuss, and I think you may be ahead of me with this, longer hours as, surprisingly, we had fallen behind again. I thought I might mention the waste of time in Portugal, but thought better of it, and I went for the tried and tested response that the crew was knackered and incapable of doing much more, but that fell on deaf ears.

It came down to a negotiation of more money for more hours. Was anyone even looking at the budget?

The tiredness of the crew, including Michael, who must have been feeling the same, was highlighted in a shot we did on the stage at Shepperton. German soldiers were being found with the life sucked out of them by the 'Evil' side, and to add spice to the shot, the stage floor was covered in a mist from a 'dry-ice' machine, which is not healthy if you lie in it too long, but this is what the extras were being asked to do.

After assurances were given that they would only be in there a matter of seconds, off we went, but with Michael, nothing was that quick and simple and a couple of minutes elapsed before the First shouted, "Cut". Gradually, every extra got up bar one, and a frantic scramble ensued to bring him round with the help of the Unit nurse. Hearts in mouths time for Production. The repercussions would have been enormous. Fortunately, he was alright, and I think he may have had a bonus in his pay packet, but his plight was down to bad decision-making by people so tired they couldn't think straight, and I did point this out to Colin. I think he agreed, but was toothless.

Out of the studios again, we were going to Wales for what turned out to be three and a half weeks of work, mostly outside in the rain. One of the main actors. Ian McKellen was supposed to discover some graphics on the wall of a mine which gave us a clue as to why all these strange happenings were going on, so we had located in a huge disused slate mine. He made startling revelations that the writing on the wall dated back over a thousand years, as per the script.

I should point out, at this point, that Standby Prop Men need to know the script as well as anyone so as not to be caught out if certain props are needed, etc. Me and my old mate Denis prided ourselves on rarely getting stuck in the proverbial by knowing the script inside out, knowing that even words can mean something we might need to get involved with.

So with this in mind, as we listened to the dialogue in the echoing slate mine, it suddenly came to me that there was something wrong with what Ian was saying. Due to previous dialogue, the writing could not be over a thousand years old. I listened again on the second take and looked at Denis. He hadn't clocked it. I looked around at the crew, and no one was reacting either, not even the Continuity Lady who monitors the script. I began to doubt myself as it wasn't really my place to pick up on script errors, way above my pay grade.

We went again, and I heard it again, and like an itch I had to scratch it, even if it made me look a complete fool, so I summoned up all my courage and went to the First before we shot again.

You could see his thoughts on my intrusion, but he went over to Michael and said he just wanted to check something. The next minute there was the Continuity Lady, the First, Michael, Ian McKellen and me, huddled around the script, checking previous dialogue.

There was a pregnant pause before the Continuity Lady finally said, "He's right! It can't be a thousand years."

Thank God for that. I could have gone down in flames, big time.

Michael looked at me. "Peter. Well done, man. Lucky someone listens to the words."

It got changed to over 500 years. So, when or if you see the film, remember when Ian McKellen delivers that line, it was me that stopped him from being labelled the worst mathematician of all time.

After that moment of fame, I had my leg pulled by everyone, even being asked on occasions, jokingly by Michael, if what was being said was ok by me and if we could carry on. It was a bit of fun, and we actually got on better after that, but I wondered if I had not said anything if anyone would have noticed the error.

We were also using the exterior of the slate mine for other shots with Scott, where he arrives at the outskirts of the Keep for the first time. As a Superhero, Scott was supposedly oblivious to the elements, feeling no cold, heat or anything else, but we were filming around November, late autumn, in a slate mine in Wales, and it was absolutely freezing. All the crew had so much protective clothing on they could hardly move, but Scott was to be standing on the edge of a windswept mine in a tee shirt and not feeling a thing. We had seen him on the boat, and he wasn't carrying a suitcase containing protective clothing, so this was one of those practical problems any scriptwriter could not easily foresee, but it was still a problem to be solved.

The Production had discussed this before the unit arrived

in Wales and had rented a cottage close to the location where he could live a spartan existence in a cold atmosphere to acclimatise himself to the elements, and so feel 'at one' with his surroundings.

So, it was now the day for shooting this sequence. We were all standing on a cliff edge near the mine, and Scott walks into shot and looks meaningfully into the distance. The wind was severe as we were so high up, and it was bitterly cold as Scott strode in wearing his tee shirt and jeans as well, obviously. He stopped and looked ahead for what was about 10 seconds before he could take it no more.

"F***ing Hell. It's freezing. Can I get a coat?" he screamed.

The crew collapsed. A whole week living frugally in a cold cottage in Wales for 10 seconds. More money wasted.

We did manage to conjure up this shot by removing his coat just before the camera turned, but it does show how script and actual can be so far apart.

After this location, we moved to our main location in Wales, near a town called Bangor. About 20 minutes from our hotels, a Romanian village had been built in a disused pit, which was only accessible by two purpose-built lifts, and this is where a mock-up of the Keep was constructed to shoot the exteriors to match the interiors we had shot in the studio.

Exterior shooting for any length of time will always throw up its problems because you are totally reliant on the weather, which can disrupt the continuity of a film on a whim. If you start in sunny climates only for it to pour down with rain, it's difficult to convince the audience that the sequences follow each other in time, so you must decide when to shoot while on location based on weather forecasts for the time you are there.

For those people who have been to Wales in late Autumn, rain is more likely than sun, and once we started, we certainly got plenty of the former. Every day and every night for over three weeks.

The move to Bangor meant we arrived at a reasonable time.

We were not shooting and were in our own time, something that we hadn't seen for what seemed an eternity. We were actually able to sit down and have a relaxing meal, and it felt unnerving thinking we should have been working instead of enjoying ourselves. The feeling of relief was evident in people, and after the meal we all drifted into the bar. Drinks started to flow, and everyone, instead of drifting off to bed, went for it. Rounds of drinks were coming from everywhere, and I was drinking stuff I hadn't even ordered along with everyone else. It seemed like a moment of madness before something bad was going to happen, and I think the pent-up frustration of the past weeks had finally vented itself in this frenzy of drinking. It went on until quite late when tiredness eventually drove everyone to their beds, and the early start in the morning certainly took its toll on an already knackered crew.

We had, as I said, established long-day work practices and this carried on here. The logistics of getting down the pit by the lifts and then out again and driving back to the hotels gnawed away at your personal time, what there was of it and with your clothing continually wet all the time, each day was an endurance test.

After a week, one of the lifts broke, never to be fixed, so our exodus every day was like trying to cram yourself into the last train out of London and to add to all this, I was once again called to see Colin. No surprise here!

Our working day had become 6am to 2am, which was madness in anyone's book, but they wanted more. I pointed out that with packing up, getting out with only one lift, driving to the hotels, trying to dry your constantly soaked clothing and then getting back was only leaving 2 to 3 hours of sleep at most. The money side of things was irrelevant; it had become a case of self-preservation. Their request to start at 5am would mean most of the crew would be driving back to the hotel just in time to turn round and come back again, and the concentration rates of all of us must have been running at about 20 per cent. Someone was likely to get killed on the roads!

At last, I got through to them, and they shelved the idea, but it meant tagging a few more days on at the end to get all we needed done before we finally left this Hell hole and returned to Shepperton. I have never seen so many relieved faces as we left Bangor.

This location over meant we had completed the 'Principal' shooting by Christmas as per the funding agreement, but the truth was the evolution of the monster from 'red sparkles' in the air to human form was far from done and needed special effects to make it work. After the Christmas break, this shooting began on a huge stage in Shepperton, known as 'H' stage, thankfully without Denis or me, and went on for a full 9 months extra. Yes, 9 months and the costs were horrendous.

It was rumoured that what was supposed to be a $10.2 million budget turned into more like $46 million, over 4 times as much, but finally this film was in the can and after editing it was put out on the circuit.

It lasted 6 days and was so badly received that they withdrew it from the circuit, and it went straight on to video, the technology of the day. I can't think of anyone who might have benefitted from this film other than the crew. I, myself, earned an absolute fortune but had not seen very much of my family and felt completely exhausted. The money, however, was to play an integral part in the next stage of our lives.

I never saw the film, although a few years back I bought an old VHS copy of it, which I haven't seen as I don't have a player for it, but I thought that was the last I would hear about the 'Keep', until some years later. About 30 years later, to be more precise, when I was contacted, out of the blue, by someone representing a company that was making a documentary about the filming of 'The Keep'.

Apparently, over the years this film had become a bit of a cult movie and had quite a following, and there was a clamour for the film to be re-edited as they felt the original cut did not show the film in its best light. Excuse me while I recompose myself.

In my opinion, it would take a lot more than a re-edit to make this film work, but each to their own, for there are films I have loved that other people hated. It is subjective, after all.

The idea was that all the crew that worked on the film and were still alive, would sit in front of a camera and be asked questions about their part in the making of 'The Keep', and this was to take place in a small studio just outside Bristol. I say 'studio' as it turned out to be a converted barn on an old farm, but hey ho.

Denis and I went together, did our bit, signed a disclaimer form and then drove home, wondering what the hell that was all about and how that would help in the re-editing of the film.

We never saw the documentary and have no idea if the new version ever came out, but for those supporters, it meant something, and there is nothing wrong with that. To Den and me, it was in the category of 'films best avoided' and one to talk about but not be seen.

I have mentioned Denis a lot so far without really explaining too much about him, and how we came to meet, so I think it only right to write a few words about someone who featured a great deal in my life both in and out of films.

CHAPTER 17

DENIS

Denis Hopperton was his full name, and we came to meet on the day that I clambered over the fence between EMI studios and Les's house on starting my first day with George on 'Great Muppet Caper'. He had worked with George well before we met and was one of his regulars.

He wasn't a tall man, but was very stocky and strong, wore a broad moustache and liked to wear his shirts with one too many buttons undone to show off his hairy chest. He'll hate me for saying that, but we are good mates, so I think I may get away with it.

He was a very charming man and easy to get on with, and it wasn't long before I realised he worked and thought a lot like me and was someone I could comfortably work with. I think George saw that and that's why we did so many pictures with him.

Our friendship on films spilled out into our social life, and very soon, Ann and I and Denis's then-wife, Claire, were seeing each other quite regularly. Claire was Canadian and a professional singer, and often our proposed meetup was postponed when she got a late-minute booking. A bit like the film industry; sometimes your life is not your own.

Den and I worked on all of George's films, and we worked so well together we even got requests from other Art Departments to work with them, 'Oliver Twist' being one of them. Let's forget that one. Our loyalties lay with George, however, as he was a good friend as well as our guv'nor and liked to do things the right way, as Denis and I did.

We had plenty of laughs on films, and being good friends got us through some of the more hairy moments, but the film industry, like with so many other professions pressurised relationships and what with Claire's chosen career as well, their marriage ended prematurely, which was a real shame as Ann and Claire had formed a real friendship. Breakups always cause awkward moments, and this was no exception.

He was sad for a while, and I think he still holds a candle for Claire, but he picked himself up and later married another lady called Carol.

Denis and I were also, along with George and Les, to form a Prop Hire company together, but more about that later. So, the three most influential people regarding my film career and I were to be linked in yet another way, with its own story to tell.

After the trials of the 'Keep', we were all exhausted, and as with the normal workings of the film industry, not a lot happens between Christmas and March, so we all rested until that itch started again, and we went seeking work to keep the money coming in. George, as always, hadn't been completely asleep and had acquired another little 'HandMade' production which was to be called 'Bullshot', a spoof version of 'Bulldog Drummond', an English forerunner of James Bond.

Another chance to meet my old mate, The Beatle, George Harrison. (He lied.) So, in April 1983, we started work on Bullshot.

CHAPTER 18

BULLSHOT

In a 1930s tearoom, Bullshot Crummond fears for the worse. He believes his arch enemy, 'The Count', is on the attack. Spotting a huge cake on the tea trolley, his mind calculates the impending peril. He launches himself on top of the cake to deaden the explosion of what he thinks is a hidden bomb, shouting, "Look out everybody, it's a 'Bomb Gateau.'"

The impact of his body sends the trolley flying across the room, smashing into the wall, and its cargo spills all over the floor. There is no explosion, for Bullshot has totally got this wrong as usual.

One scene from 'Bullshot' which illustrates the sheer madness of our hero, who, despite making a mess of everything he attempts, ends up righting wrong and defeating the evil Count.

This wasn't a big production and, in the end, didn't turn out to be a great box office success, but it had some good old comedy actors, such as Mel Smith, Billy Connolly, etc., in it and a silly slapstick style script about an evil arch-villain and a crusading goody-goody and was set in the 1930s.

It had all the makings of success with the popular duo of Dick Clement as director and Ian La Frenais producing. They had made their names in some really funny TV productions and were now being given their chance on the big screen.

Written by three of the main actors, Ron House, Dizzy White and Alan Shearman, and based on a Broadway production, it set the villain, Count Otto von Bruno, against the hero, Bullshot Crummond, in a plot about a mad professor and a machine he had made.

Mel Smith played the henchman to the 'Count' who was played by Ron, and they didn't get on at all well. Ron had all the lines, Mel had very few, so had resorted to standing behind Ron, making a whole string of grimaces and facial expressions to enhance his part, often while Ron was doing his best acting. He did it so well that it made Ron's role look very ordinary, and he could see he was being outdone by Mel and was not best pleased.

Consequently, one day after a sequence with Ron speaking and Mel clowning, he could take it no longer, so went over to confront him.

"Mel, I've just spoken to Dick, and he doesn't want you to do those faces anymore," Ron said.

"Why? Are you going to do them?" Mel said quick as a flash and walked off.

Ron stood there speechless, and the crew, who had all overheard this, had to try and stop themselves from laughing, despite it being funny. It did rather set the tone for the rest of the picture.

Alan did his best to help his character by getting out of ludicrous situations with a series of funny stances and hand movements to show how he was assessing angles, trajectories, distances, etc. It was great comedy, and he delivered some very funny lines, including one when he is wearing only his 'Long-Johns' underwear with a huge sock stuffed down where his privates are while his friend, 'Binkie', watches him getting dressed.

With Binkie looking at the 'bulge' in amazement, he delivers the line, "Between you and I, Binkie, I think there's something big coming up."

Binkie, eying the 'package', nods in agreement.

As you can imagine, there were plenty of gunshots and explosions, where professional armourers and special effects were used to supervise and carry out these sequences. Most went well except on one occasion in a teashop scene where Bullshot is pursuing the villain and, believing he is under attack, we see teacups, saucers and teapots exploding after being hit by stray bullets. The crowd extras were to panic and run off in fear, and all was going well until one take when a bit of a china teapot flew off and hit one of the extras in the face. To her credit, she touched her face briefly and carried on with the action so as not to spoil the shot, but it had obviously hurt her.

The nurse tended to her, and she was ok, but if you ever see this sequence look out for the mishap in the background.

It wasn't a long film but got panned by the critics, one saying that the plot was so far-fetched as to be unbelievable. Hadn't he realised it was a comical spoof?

I watched it and liked it, but it goes back to what I said about the 'Keep'; it all comes down to personal taste.

Sad for HandMade, they needed the success, but I was to work with them later on a film called 'Water'. Not every film was a 'Star Wars', but it doesn't mean they shouldn't be made.

Compared to the 'Keep', this had been very pleasant to work on, and I got home quite a lot, which was always a good thing. We were settling well into our new house, and the girls were growing up well and making friends locally. It's funny when you are desperate to make a move, as we were up from Folkestone, how you don't always see the downside of the house you buy. Don't get me wrong, we loved the house, and it enabled us to make a positive change in our lives, and I was home a lot more despite having to be away so much, but with the girls growing, we were beginning to see the limitations of our home. The front garden was small, and the back wasn't massive, and at the end of the garden, we realised there was a drop down to a railway line. Amazingly, we hadn't noticed that when we bought it, but only after when we could hear the trains going by.

It altered our view on what we wanted to do to the house, as it became clear that we would most likely move again and best to do this before the girls started school properly.

I'd had a few weeks off after 'Bullshot', and in the summer months, so I was able to spend some decent time taking Ellie and Ria out, but then as I returned from a lovely day out with my family, the phone rang.

It was George. He had been offered a picture starting in a couple of weeks, if I was interested. Of course, I was, although it meant breaking up this idyllic time at home, but if I thought what was going to happen, did happen, I was going to need as much work as I could.

It was a film called 'The Razor's Edge' and starred the American comedian Bill Murray, playing his first serious role as an actor. There was some shooting in this country and some abroad in France, Switzerland, Belgium and India, meaning I would have another stint away from home. So, in July 1983, I headed off to start the next film.

CHAPTER 19

THE RAZOR'S EDGE

Bill Murray stands thoughtfully on the bow of a small wooden boat making its way down a wide Asian river as part of his tour of self-discovery through Europe and Asia. This is a man that has served in the First World War, seen the horror of conflict, and now wants to know who he is and what he wants to do with his life. A story of romance, deception, sacrifice and discovery.

This was a first world war-based film, where Bill is a returning soldier trying to come to terms with the memories of the blood-stained battlefields he has just left and how his life was affected by it. He postpones his impending wedding and goes on a soul-searching tour of self-discovery in Europe and Asia. Quite a depressing film in some respects, but very poignant.

He had other actors with him, including Catherine Hicks, Theresa Russell and Denholm Elliott, and the film won Bill acclaim for his performance. I personally wondered what film they had been watching because it wasn't the one I worked on. I found him very wooden and mostly had one expression on his face, delivering every line in one tone. Just as well I'm not a film critic, I suppose.

Listening to the dialogue was hard going, but the crew, as usual, lifted the mood, made each day enjoyable, and we had a few laughs. While we were in France, the true unity of the crew came through, and in Paris that unity was to be tested by the French crew working alongside us.

Call me an old cynic, but during my career, I found there was always an 'us and them' attitude when you were working with a foreign crew in their country. They were always polite, and there was an appreciation of what the other was doing, but you never really mix, and there is a type of rivalry going on.

This was the case in Paris. I am not sure the French really like the English very much anyway, so we started from a low base. We would pass the time of day, but you forever felt things were being said about us in their own language so we wouldn't understand.

We had been there a few days, and amongst the men there was the inevitable talk about football, which got more and more heated after a couple of beers. The French thought English football was crap, and we had the same thoughts about them. One night, out of this drunken debate, a challenge was laid down by the French to have a match between the English and French crews. Honours go to the winners. How could we resist such a challenge? So plans were laid to get our finest team on the pitch.

None of us had ever stepped onto the field together, let alone as a team representing the honour of English football, and we didn't even know if any of us could play or in what position. Having taken the proverbial gauntlet from the floor, we had to find a way to weld together a team worthy of our country, although, in the cold light of day, we might have slightly been regretting our bravado.

We started to write the names down of the willing participants and what position they played in, and it was astounding the number of goalscoring centre forwards we had, how few defenders came forward and not a single goalkeeper. This was a very unbalanced setup, but we had 16 gladiators willing to die for their country, and after some persuasion, we talked two of the taller men into taking a spell in goal, although they weren't happy about it.

The big day came, and the crowds massed around the artificial pitch in the middle of Paris to witness this spectacle. Well, a few people came anyway. None of us had a proper kit, only what we could throw together in as near one matching colour as we could muster. We were here, after all, to make a film, not play football. In stark contrast, our opponents ran onto the pitch in immaculate blue and white kit, looking like a real athletic team.

It was funny, but I hardly recognised any of the faces from the crew we had been working with, but it didn't seem relevant at the time.

To our amazement, just before we were going to kick off, a surprise guest arrived wanting to play in goal. It was Bill Murray himself, fully kitted out and wearing proper football boots. He looked the part and saved our 'tall' volunteers the embarrassment of going 'between the sticks'.

This was back in the 1980s when football in America was in its early stages, so we weren't even sure if Bill knew the rules, but he was raring to go, so what the hell.

I am not sure many of us had played on an artificial pitch before, and they do take some getting used to, with the ball bouncing all over the place. The French settled much quicker than us and were obviously accustomed to it. Within 5 minutes, we were two goals down. They were taking us apart. There is nothing worse than the wounded pride of a would-be English footballer, so in went the big sliding tackles and the subtle trips, stemming the tide for a while, but we hadn't mustered one attack yet. Bill, to his credit, had made a couple of decent saves; it was just our band of goalscoring centre forwards that seemed to have disappeared.

Then Fate stepped in. A speculative punt down the middle took an uncanny bounce and went straight over the French goalkeeper's head into the net. It was 2-1, and we were back in it, or so we thought. It only served to rile the French, and 2 minutes later, they scored again, then again, then again. By half time we were 7-1 down and feeling mighty sorry for ourselves. We were knackered, and our legs were torn to shreds from sliding on the artificial surface as we sucked on our slices of orange. We had to have them!

The French team wasn't even out of breath and were waiting eagerly to come back on to complete the humiliation. After another pitiful display in the second half, we left the pitch, heads bowed, having been slaughtered 12-2. The honours had most equivocally gone to the French. Were we that bad, or was something not right here? The answer to that came a couple of days later when we found out that our opponents had no French crew in it at all, but in fact were a semi-professional side brought in as 'ringers' to teach us bragging Brits a lesson.

As a footnote, Bill did not let in the 12 goals as he was substituted at 8-1 when the producer Harry Benn found out his leading actor was throwing himself around on an artificial pitch in front of marauding French forwards. Not sure the film's insurance would take kindly if he were injured and filming had to stop.

Still, I do get to say I played in Paris on the same team as Bill Murray, despite the score-line; and having found out about the 'ringers', we demanded a rematch, which happened a few days later. This time we had rules that said you couldn't play unless your name was on the official crew list. We were not going to be caught out a second time, and in a completely different type of match, we found our goalscoring centre forwards again and won 5-2. Bill wasn't allowed to play. He'd had his moment of glory. Harry had quashed that idea.

We had some other strange episodes in Paris, like when

we built a long market that Bill and his friends had to walk through, giving their dialogue. We had dressed it with fresh produce and meat but never finished shooting it as we had to be somewhere else, and so we closed up the wood fronts and left it until we came back, which turned out to be two weeks later. The food was rotting and stank, but we had nothing else, so after shooting we got skips to dump it in. As we were leaving, crowds of people were in there grabbing what they could. It was terrible to see how desperate they were, having to resort to this, but we couldn't stop them, so let it go on. A lasting memory I wish I hadn't witnessed.

True to form with Harry, being known for his tightness, he managed to ease Denis and me out of any more foreign locations, choosing to use the Production Designer as the stand-in Prop man. Not at all surprising!

There were some pick-up shots in the studio after the locations, which resulted in one howler that can be seen in the film. Bill is supposedly on the top of a mountain, speaking, and there is no cold breath coming out of his mouth as it was shot in a warm set. Harry wouldn't go back to the location to reshoot it, so it stayed.

It wasn't the greatest film you'll see, but Harry was a shrewd producer, and he got his money back at the box office, which is what he was paid to do.

I had put another notch on my career pole and went home to see my family again, thinking that was me done for the year, but George had other ideas, and it wasn't long before we were prepping for another film.

While at home, Ann and I talked more about the house we were living in. It was ok for now, but I think we both agreed it was never going to be our forever home, and although we couldn't afford to do it now, we would have to eventually, so we decided the big plans we had for this house would be shelved and the bare minimum spent on it. It needed a new kitchen, so we invested in one we really liked, and when you see it looking so nice, you question whether you do need to move. There was another consideration, the girls' schooling. Ellie was coming up to 5 and a half years old, and soon we would have to think about what school she would go to. I know it sounds snobbish, but the State schools in our area did not have a good reputation, and as a result of that, there was an abundance of private schools available. There was money in the area, so these schools prospered.

Ria was just over two, so it didn't matter for her so much at the moment, but these decisions need some planning ahead, and after some research and financial calculations, we decided on a school that we thought would be good for Ellie.

This was another financial obligation, but you only have one go at your child's schooling, and we wanted to get it right, so we took steps to make it happen.

It was becoming clear to me that Ria's schooling would probably go the same way, and if we were going to move house, I needed to start earning money again, and a lot of it. We were going to need it!

Fortunately, as I said, George had done his best work, and not long after finishing on 'The Razor's Edge', we started on a film called 'Brazil', based at Wembley studios, my old hunting ground. I couldn't wait to get going and start filling the 'schooling and moving' fund.

CHAPTER 20

BRAZIL

We close in on an old printing machine, with the distinct sound of a fly buzzing about. The machine is printing a list of 'terrorist' names on official paperwork, and as it taps away, the fly falls into the mechanism, making it jump and print the wrong letter. Now, a completely innocent man will, from now on, be hunted at all costs until he is found and punished.

The film is 'Brazil', directed by another Monty Python member, Terry Gilliam, an American with a real zany sense of humour, and stars Jonathan Pryce in the main role, aided by so many other great actors, including his old mate Michael Palin from the Python years and a cameo role for Robert De Niro.

It was set sometime in the future when the State is in total control of everyone's lives, and paperwork is essential for you to do anything. Any misdemeanour is met with a knock on the door and a short drive to a detention centre. No debate.

I had worked with a large number of actors at this point in my career, and it was always an enjoyable part for me to strike up a good relationship with them, but I hadn't realised how close a relationship that would be with Robert.

Before any film, there is a lot of preparation work, and with a film like this set in the future but with a definite look of the past, it was important to strike a balance. Robert was desperate to be in this film for some reason and initially wanted to play the part of a character called Jack Lint, but this had already been given to Michael, so he reluctantly accepted the role of Harry Tuttle, a freelance heating engineer. This was a much smaller role, but as with the way of Robert, he was determined to make it a memorable one and set about building his character.

As a freelance heating engineer, he had to flit in and out of buildings doing work without the statutory form 27B/6 required by the Department of Public Works and set about amassing a huge range of various tools to make him look the part. Just a side note, this film was conceived by an idea Terry had based on the book by George Orwell called '1984', and throughout the film, there are all sorts of references to it. The number 27B/6 is a reference to George Orwell himself, who lived in Canterbury Square, Apartment no 27B on the sixth floor. Anyway, I digress.

To facilitate Robert's appetite for new tools, George Ball, not Orwell, had to bring in masses of equipment for Robert to come and view in the Prop room and decide which ones he thought useful. George brought in hundreds and hundreds of items before Robert had enough for his vision. To be fair, Robert paid for all the tools himself, but his fussiness for detail was becoming apparent.

Terry's initial enthusiasm for Robert being on the film even turned to utter frustration as his severe attention to detail began to disrupt the film, and he was quoted as saying he'd like to strangle him sometimes.

With most actors, a few takes would be necessary, whereas Robert would just keep going on and on for 25 to 30 takes. He had built his dialogue around the actions while he was repairing the heating equipment in a flat and had made it so complicated that if he made a mistake with either the action or the dialogue, he would stop and want to go again. He was only supposed to be shooting for one week, but all the delays turned this into two.

He had likened his work in the film to that of a brain surgeon and had a large magnifying glass attached to his head to show the similarities. Really?

The interior of the flat where Robert is supposedly doing his work was built on a set at Wembley and was a double-skinned wall to provide depth when Robert takes a panel off to look inside at the workings.

We were supposed to shoot his scenes in the morning, but as we got started on his intricate action/dialogue mix, it became clear that this wasn't going to happen. He got so far, then made a slip, and we would go again. His action was to lean inside the wall and pull on an old part, but he said he didn't feel right unless he had something tangible to pull against, and could he have someone holding his arm in the wall to make it look right? Be fair; who else was that going to be? Yep, me!

To gain access to this position, I had to climb down from the top of the wall and wedge myself inside the panel where I could grab his arm and release it at the right moment. This would have normally been a few takes, but this was all being shot as one continuous sequence, as I said. It was not the most comfortable place to be stuck in, and extremely hot with no ventilation and all the sparks' lights blaring.

There was mistake after mistake, and you could see the frustration building up in Robert, to the point where Terry had had enough and said we should break early for lunch and let Robert collect his thoughts. It was heaven getting out of my heated ventilation shaft, but short-lived, as I knew I would be back in there straight after lunch. Down I went and, on his arm I pulled, and finally he got it right. I don't know who was more relieved, him or me. I had been in that wall for a total of

6 hours. 6 hours!

So, my claim to fame is if you see 'Brazil' and watch the scene where Robert is struggling to repair the heating in the flat, that's me inside the wall pulling his arm.

Robert never got to do the close-ups of his hands, as Terry did it himself, deciding he didn't have the time to let Robert have a go. I think he was glad this part of the film was over, and he could return to normal a bit more. Robert appeared only once more in the film when we were doing the exteriors for the flat. After his work is finished, he leaves and zip wires down a 14-storey building, which he clearly wasn't allowed to do himself.

This was done with a 1-inch high lead figure dropping down a 2-foot-high model of the building. Sorry to spoil it for you.

The building itself was in Paris in a huge apartment complex called 'Marne la Vallee', and its design was something to be marvelled at. It had two great 14-storey towers, like chimneys, joined at the base by an enclosed tunnel and the wind draft down through this complex was horrendous, causing freezing blasts of air if you were anywhere inside, dropping the temperature far lower than outside. It was warmer to go outside than to stay in. We were only working inside, and all of the crew had been caught out as to the type of clothing we should bring and so were layered up with anything we brought with us. The catering had to keep supplying us with hot soup and drinks to keep us going; it was so cold.

I am not sure I have ever worked in a colder environment, and everyone was so relieved when we finally left to return to England to do studio and location work.

One location turned into a horror show for the crew due to Terry's love of 'atmosphere' in the form of smoke, dust, and any other foul substance he could muster up.

We were shooting between two disused buildings, with the camera at one end of the 'alley', looking at the action coming in our direction. All the crew were behind the camera, and Terry had asked for 'atmosphere', so we had smoke machines, dust machines and burning tyres all blasting down our way.

Gradually hoods on coats went up, then scarves across your face, until you couldn't see a thing and were blindly breathing in all the acrid smoke from the tyres. Finally, it stopped, and we could breathe again, but as we removed our hoods and scarves, the outlines were revealed in a black tarry mass on our faces which didn't rub off. Out came the creams and wet wipes but with little effect, and we all walked round like we had 'Lone Ranger' masks on.

All our clothes stank of smoke and tar and, to all intents and purposes, were ruined. There were a few disgruntled people on the unit, and this spilled over to the next day at the studios when all the complaints started pouring into Production. They called a crew meeting where they were questioned about compensation for the ruined clothing and possible long-term health effects of breathing in the 'atmosphere'. They couldn't do much about the health problems, but everyone got an allowance to buy new clothing, so honours even, but we didn't do any more sequences like that.

There were many dream sequences in the film, one involving a huge 'Samurai' warrior, reflective of Terry's love of Akira Kurosawa's Japanese movies. The man inside the suit was a big black actor whose knees were a bit dodgy and, because of his weight and the weight of the costume, he wasn't able to stand for too long. After every take, we had to provide him with a stool to sit on, which posed the question of why he was chosen in the first place with so many problems to contend with.

A lot of the detail and manner of the film came from the personal experiences and observations of Terry, and the format of the film certainly shows his quirky nature. He struggled with the name of the film, discarding 'The Ministry', 'The Ministry of Torture', 'So that's why the Bourgeoisie sucks' and even '1984 ½', but that one was dropped because it might have too many legal complications. Finally, after sitting on a beach in the UK, when the weather wasn't very good, Terry spotted a man listening and singing the famous song 'Brazil', and saw he was enjoying himself so much despite the inclement conditions that it inspired him to call his film after the song.

The rest of the film is littered with little details.

There is a creepy mask that Michael Palin wears, and it apparently was inspired by a mask Terry's mum had given him. Now you know where Terry got his strangeness from.

The bombings in a restaurant were inspired by the IRA bombings in London, where Terry lived. The film was inspired by George Orwell's book 1984, although Terry admits he had never read it. Funnily enough, the film was shot in 1984. Now there's a thing!

When Sam Lowry, the main character, played by Jonathon, goes to see Jack Lint, the elevator in 'The Information Retrieval' building goes up to floor 84 as in 1984.

There are probably even more than this, but this is just a taster.

With all the problems of making the films, you would think that Terry would be happy to get on and show it to the public, but he hadn't foreseen what else he would have to contend with to get it in the cinemas. The 20-week shooting schedule turned into 9 months with all the special effects and dream sequences to be shot after principal shooting finished, and he was determined to get on and film what he had conceived in his mind, which put him under a lot of stress. It was rumoured that the pressure got to him so much that the stress caused him to lose all feeling in his legs for a week.

His problems didn't end there. The top man at Universal studios, Sid Sheinberg, didn't like Terry's cut of the film and refused to release it, with the dispute becoming very heated and very public.

Terry produced a picture of Sid on a TV interview and told the viewers that 'this man' had stopped the release of his film and went further by taking an ad out in a theatrical magazine called 'Daily Variety', which cost him $1500 at the time and was bordered like a funeral invitation saying, "Dear Sid Sheinberg. When are you going to release my film?" Signed Terry Gilliam.

Universal themselves went on to re-edit their own version in the form of love conquers all, but copies of Terry's cut were circulating Hollywood to rave reviews, and critics were saying it should be up for 'Best Picture' Oscar. Universal relented, and his cut hit the cinemas.

When you think of all the things he had to go through, it sort of puts your own problems into perspective. At the end of the day, we could pack up and go home knowing there was a cheque in the post. No such luck for Terry. He threw his whole existence into that movie.

There was a spin-off that would come from working on this film that I could never have foreseen. One night when Denis and I were driving back from a location shoot, tired and wanting to get home, we started talking about our futures. Whether it was the weariness that was making us think this way, I don't know, but we had thoughts of doing something else than what we were doing and began to explore the possibilities.

One idea that did come up was starting our own Prop Hire business. It was what we knew a great deal about. We knew an awful lot of buyers and Art Department people that might come to us, and as we brainstormed the prospect, the more the seed started to grow in our minds. We couldn't, at that moment, think of the type of props we would hire as most things had already been covered, but as we went on, we decided that although it was all covered, the standard of the hire companies was not high and could be improved. The more we thought about it, the more likely it seemed a good plan, and soon we were hammering out details and decided that to spread the financial load and the burden of running it, we would need another partner.

The obvious choice would be George, so we parked the thought and waited until the following day to discuss it with him.

CHAPTER 21

1984

George Orwell certainly got it right, in my case, when he wrote his book '1984' predicting all sorts of changes in society, because I was to find out that this year was going to be very eventful for me and ultimately would change the course of my life.

I was already working on a film in 1984, which drew its concept from the '1984' book; that, in itself, was strange, and here I was discussing a possible project that would take me out of the film industry, an industry that had given me so much. I wondered why I was having such thoughts, why I felt so unsettled, and why I needed such a change in my life. Maybe I finally had had enough of being away so much, not seeing my girls growing up, not doing enough with Ann and not having more time to do the things I liked to do; who knows? All I knew was that now this idea was out there, I didn't want to let it go.

The next day, Denis and I went into the Prop room and spoke to George about our project. He wasn't very interested, and we felt he was quite content with his lot and didn't want to upset the apple cart. No matter; Denis and I thought about it, and Les's name came up. In my experience, he had always been up for putting his money into ventures, so we had high hopes he would say yes.

Les wasn't keen either. Den and I thought we could still do it on our own, so we set about making plans to find suitable premises in a location that would be right in the heart of 'Prop Hire Land'.

We were still working on 'Brazil', so there wasn't a great deal of time for us to start looking, and for a day or so, we didn't get very far. Then one morning as we entered the Prop room, George announced he had thought about our proposal and had changed his mind. He was in and said that on the way home, he had spotted an industrial unit up for lease that was in an ideal location, and we should go and look at it. He had also come up with a name. 'ALLPROPS'. Here was George doing what he always did and taking charge, but this was great news and reassuring to have such an able partner. I went home really excited and couldn't wait to tell Ann. As we sat down to dinner, the phone rang. It was Les, and he too had changed his mind and wanted in. The problem was, we hadn't told Les we had asked George and vice versa, and although they had worked with each other, they weren't the best of mates. I couldn't say we didn't need him any more after all he had done for me, so I had to diplomatically drop George's name as another partner and wait for his reaction. Unbelievably, he was ok with it, so I had to tell Denis and George we were now 4.

It didn't go as badly as I thought it might, so we all set about getting this started as soon as we could, and estimated to get going we would have to put in about £3000 each. I personally couldn't afford to do this, but it was such an opportunity I decided I would raise the money in whatever way I could, so I booked an appointment with the Bank Manager of the bank I had been with for 20 years, thinking it would be no problem.

It was. They would only lend me £2700 based on my figures. I couldn't believe it. They wouldn't even budge when I offered them the account of our new business, so in frustration, I went across the road to another bank, with the smug grin of my bank manager firmly fixed in my mind. It took a while to convince them, but eventually we did a deal, and I had great satisfaction telling my existing bank where to stick it.

Within a few months we were up and running, and this was all going on while we were still working on films. It was a really hectic time and very stressful, but exciting, nevertheless. All we had to do was make this work, and that was to bring us an awful lot more problems, as I will explain a little later. For now, we had to finish 'Brazil' and keep in work to pay for all of this, because we would have to fund our 'baby' for quite a few years, we were to find out.

Les was to come to my rescue again. George didn't have anything yet to follow 'Brazil', but Les had been offered a film that went to St Lucia as one of its locations, and they were even allowing the crew to take their families with them for a small contribution. An opportunity not to miss, so I bit his hand off. This was a film starring Michael Caine, called 'Water'.

CHAPTER 22

WATER

Leonard Rossiter, dressed in his pinstripe suit and bowler hat, carrying the compulsory briefcase, disembarks from the launch bringing him to the tropical island of 'Cascara'. Michael Caine, dressed in full white military uniform, salutes him with a sword that nearly swipes Leonard, who recoils in horror. He has come to take back the flag as Britain is withdrawing from the island.

If you like a light-hearted, Caribbean comedy film starring a host of brilliant and funny actors, then this is a film for you.

It was another HandMade Films production with Dick and Ian at the helm, with some great comedy actors in the cast. George Harrison was executive producer. We, obviously, nodded to each other.

As well as Michael, there was Billy Connolly, Fulton Mackay, Leonard Rossiter, and Fred Gwynne, to name but a few and had all the makings of a good, funny film.

On a mythical island called Cascara, there is a disused oil rig that is found to be producing mineral water of a high grade and containing a special laxative that makes you 'shit like clockwork'. It is owned by a multinational company called 'Spenco', but the Islanders want the newfound product to benefit them, and so Billy Connolly, playing the part of a revolutionary named 'Delgado', leads a fight against the corporation. A French mineral water company also becomes interested, and the sleepy island is sleepy no more. Michael, who plays the British Governor of the island, gets embroiled in all this with the resulting chaos.

Fred Gwynne, the renowned 'Munster's' star, heads up Spenco and delivers some great lines, including, "Spenco strides the world like some colossus, not like some faggot with a glass of mineral water and a twist." Don't know why that line is so effective, but it did catch on around the unit.

As with 'Brazil', there were hidden bits of humour in this film. The name Cascara is, in fact, the name of a plant that has laxative properties of its own, for example. See what I mean?

One of the other reasons that this film was a good choice for me was that Les had got together a really good team of Prop Men, most of whom were old mates I had known for years and who were all, in their own ways, very able. You could rely on any one of them if you needed a hand.

There was Denis, Johnny Palmer, who helped me become a Prop Man, Gary Dawson, who I had known since I was 10 years old playing football back in Borehamwood, and Barry Arnold, such a nice man who never stopped smiling.

All the Prop men had brought their families, so this was going to be a special time for us all and a lot of fun. While we were working, all the wives and kids were having a wonderful time, as if on holiday, and then we could all get together in the evenings.

St. Lucia was not a rich island, with only three main towns and had very limited film-making facilities, which meant everything we might need for the shoot had to be brought in large containers from England. This involved a huge amount of planning before we left our shores to make sure we had everything we could think of and more. What we didn't bring, we would have to try and find on the island.

With only three towns, the accommodation for such a large unit was limited, so we split into two distinct groups. The elite and cast in superb hotels near the main location of Soufriere, the riffraff in a hotel near the airport that had been shut for years but which had been opened just for us for the 3 or so weeks we were there. I have to say it did look as if it had been shut for a while. The distance of our 'hotel' from Soufriere meant it was a drive each morning, and the route showed the island's poverty, with people living in tin huts like bus stops right next to the roads. So sad!

As I said, our hotel was pretty basic, and the food range was quite limited, with a local banana called Plantain very prominent on a lot of the menus. Even a local restaurant, and there weren't many of those, had a menu that read 'boiled Plantain, roasted Plantain, stewed Plantain, grilled Plantain' and nothing else. If you could have thought of another way of cooking Plantain, I am sure they would have obliged. I haven't eaten Plantain since leaving the island.

It was so hot in St. Lucia that all meals were taken out on the veranda of the hotel, and as the evening light faded and the crew approached the restaurant, there were a lot of crunching sounds. When a light was shone on the ground, it revealed thousands of crawling insects which we were unknowingly trampling on as we arrived. We soon learned to bring torches to find our way through, but to be fair, we were the intruders. They were there long before us.

After a few days settling in and checking we had everything we had packed back in England; it was time to start shooting, for anything else we wanted was governed by 'Island Rules'. That is to say, a shake of the hand, a small prayer and hope to God it turned up on time, for timekeeping was obviously not taught as part of the school curriculum on St Lucia. Most people were so laid back they were positively prostrate.

Soon, we learned to lie about the time we needed things and bring it forward an hour just to get it there on time. You can't make a film and keep a schedule playing by those rules. Time is money, as I have said. What we did find was that there was no shortage of willing volunteers coming forward to be extras on the film. The lack of work on the island, with a film crew coming to them with money to spend, was like manna from heaven, and they all wanted a part of it while it was there for the taking. There was clear anger when some of them were not required while others were chosen, and many a tussle took place as a result.

With no film structure on the island, if you wanted something, you had to find someone who knew a man who might have what you want, but they couldn't see him until later, if you see where I am going with this. Generally, a bit slapdash. This was illustrated so well when we required some chickens that we needed to place on a road as a vehicle comes racing in, and they all scatter. That old shot. No chickens were killed in the making of this film, by the way, only the ones provided by the catering department.

Our location manager had asked around for us and been told that someone knew a man who lived up in the hills and kept chickens, and might be interested in hiring them to us, but he wasn't able to see him until the evening. (See what I mean.) He was happy to do it, and we gave him a time to be there, but even with our minus 1-hour St Lucia time adjustment, he was still late, but at least we had some chickens. After the first take, we found we had a big problem. Being by the coast, all of the houses were built off the ground in case of flooding, and when the chickens scattered, a lot of them disappeared under the houses, and they didn't want to come out. Can't blame them for that. Would you want to be continually charged by a speeding vehicle?

Every time we rounded them up, we were short a few. He had told us he had brought 60 chickens with him, and we had taken his word for it, not really having time to count them all. After shooting was finished, he said that he had lost a number of chickens and wanted us to pay for them. We needed him later on, so a figure was agreed upon, and he went off with his mate.

As we headed to our car to return to the hotel, we noticed our two handlers down a side street loading their chickens on to a pick-up truck, and for some reason when they saw us, they hastened their operation and sped off in the truck. Very strange.

We worked it out that during takes, his mate had been holding back some of the chickens that had gone under the houses and made it seem as if they had been lost. They came with 60 and left with 60. We had been taken for a ride, but the next time round, we would be ready. It was a ploy to get a bit more money while the film unit was here, and everyone we dealt with seemed to have their own angle on the scams, so a few days later we needed the 'chicken man' again, and he was very eager to oblige.

We were paying him per chicken, so the more he brought, the more he made. It was important, therefore, for us to know how many there were this time. This time we checked.

"Have you brought all of your chickens?" I asked.

"Me got everyone that me have," he replied.

"And how many is that?" I went on.

"60." He smiled.

"So, you have bought some more then?" I laid the trap.

"No, man, what you saying?" He looked confused.

"Well, last time you lost some which we paid you for, and you arrived with 60 that time, so you must have bought some more if you have 60 now," I smugly replied.

There was a silence while the wheels turned in his head. In that split second, he knew we had rumbled him and his mate, but he was desperately trying to think of an answer, and finally, he came out with an excuse that no one, even him, believed.

"Yeah, that's right, so I borrowed some from me neighbour."

Les, who had been listening to all this, cut in.

"Right! Well, anyway, we'll take better care of the chickens this time, won't we, so none will go missing."

I think our man got the drift and knew his plan wouldn't work a second time, so when the chickens were counted at the end of the shoot, there was, amazingly, 60 of them. Job done!

At the beginning of shooting, many actors like to establish a hand prop that defines their character for the rest of the film, and this is where standby props come in, to provide these items.

Fulton Mackay was playing the local vicar who had a drinking problem, and he had approached me to see if we had a half bottle of whiskey he could carry with him that would go in the pocket of his jacket, so I looked around and found the very thing which I filled. Obviously, not real whiskey but 'prop' whiskey made from watered-down coca cola.

He was very pleased by this as it fitted perfectly in his pocket and made him feel he had enhanced his character. After a few takes of him taking it in and out of his pocket, the mixture was starting to get shaken up a bit. We were about to go again, and he had placed the bottle back in his jacket when there was a loud 'pop'. The bottle had exploded in his pocket and spilled the entire contents all over the jacket, but the confines of the jacket had stopped the glass from flying everywhere and possibly harming him.

Quickly, the garment was ripped off him, and the Wardrobe department frantically set about trying to clean the jacket.

In the extreme heat, the bubbles in the coke had built up, and the pressure in the bottle had nowhere to go, so it had just exploded outwards.

I felt awful. I hadn't foreseen this, and nor had anyone else, I suspect, but I had nearly taken the actor out on the first day. I couldn't apologise enough, but Fulton was very gracious, and we laughed about it. The stain on the jacket was now the problem, but fate had played its trump card again and got me out of the proverbial.

Dick actually liked the stain and wanted to keep it, as he thought the drunken vicar's clothes should look more like that and not pristine. Watch it on film; that stain is all my own work, albeit by accident.

Billy Connolly was a great favourite on HandMade films as one of the executive producers, Denis O'Brien, thought he was the funniest thing on two legs and wanted him in everything, to the point where he was cast even before Michael Caine. So, a lot of the time, you could see Billy laughing and joking with everyone, and one day he came over to chat to a few of the props as we were having a break for tea. Within seconds he had gone into a routine, and we couldn't stop laughing, feeling very honoured he had chosen to talk to us.

However, a short while later, on my way to the prop truck, I went past a few of the crew who were also talking to Billy, and the dialogue from him seemed vaguely familiar. They were the same jokes and lines he had told us, and I realised he was going round testing, which went down well and which didn't, so he could hone his performance using us as guinea pigs. Cheeky monkey!

Another funny man on the cast, but whose attitude to the crew was a complete contrast to Billy's was Leonard Rossiter, who had done a string of British TV comedies and was quite a household name in the UK. Initially, his role as 'Sir Malcolm' was earmarked for John Cleese, but John didn't want to do it, so Leonard took over.

Sir Malcolm was a representative from the British Home Office and had come to the island to oversee the Governor's departure from the island as the Embassy was to be closed. He is to secure the 'flag' and return home with it.

Denis and I were preparing our stuff for this scene by the docks when Leonard arrived on his own, looking a little confused and babbling to himself. He wasn't sure what was happening next and was looking for Dick to explain it to him. Dick wasn't there then, but it didn't stop Leonard calling out his name as if he were at his beck and call. I thought I might be able to help, so I approached him.

"Sorry, Leonard, this is where the flag is taken down, presented to you by the Governor, and you take it and board the boat," I said.

Obviously, I wasn't helping as he looked at me as if I was something he'd just found on his shoe.

"I don't take instructions from the crew. Where's Dick?" he said.

From behind us came Dick's voice. "I'm right here. What's the problem, Leonard?"

"Well. Nobody has told me what I'm doing next," he said angrily.

In a calm, reassuring voice Dick spoke. "Right, this is the part where the flag is taken down, presented to you by the Governor, and you take it and board the boat. I think Peter just said that, didn't he? You should listen to the Prop Men; they know everything that's going on."

He threw me a wry old smile and walked off, leaving Leonard looking rather foolish.

Leonard may have been a good actor, but he went down in my estimations that day and marred what had been a very nice shoot so far, but things would change on that front.

I had noticed, in particular, that the camera crew did rather think they were a class above and didn't fraternise with the rest of us, and there were rumours going around that some of the cast didn't get on very well with each other.

The atmosphere on the island turned slightly sour, and you felt people were tolerating each other just to get through the shoot. The Prop Men and their families, however, had a great time, and it was a real holiday for the families. Ellie and Ria, I know, loved it and were sad to leave. We did take them back some years later.

The shoot finished in St Lucia, and we all packed our gear and headed back to England to shoot in Shepperton but also at Hartland Point in Devon, where we were shooting the exteriors of the oil rig and surrounding land. These were to match the interiors we had shot on the island, but one problem we had was that in Devon there weren't a lot of black people who we could call upon as extras, so a solution had to be found for this.

The idea was that the production would hire black extras in Bristol, not that far away, and bus them into the location each day. This worked for a while until the very last day when we needed the extras.

There had been a dispute between the Production and the Extras Agency about pay, and they wanted a better deal that they were not going to be given. Stalemate! They knew they were needed, but HandMade couldn't afford the increase, so the buses turned up to find no one waiting.

This was supposed to have been a big celebration on the hillside by the islanders after their victory over the Capitalists, and people are dancing and singing and generally enjoying the moment. Except, we didn't have anyone to dance and sing any more.

Our schedule had locked us in to do this shot, so something had to be done. Eventually, insanity stepped forward, and a ludicrous solution was concocted to use everyone on the crew who wasn't essential to that shot to be the 'crowd' on the hill. We dressed ourselves in colourful Caribbean clothes from the wardrobe department and did our best to sing and dance like Cascaran islanders. We tightened the shots as there weren't that many of us and shot from a distance so as not to see much detail, but we got it done to the delight of the Production.

It was completely silly, but sometimes that's what you have to do to make a film, so I can say I was one of the daft nutters going mad on the hillside.

The Production had also saved themselves some money by not paying all the extras for one day, so we were all treated to a few beers that night, on the house.

This would be one of the last days on location, and when the First finally said, 'It's a wrap on this location', we started to clear the set as the porta cabins we had hired to use as Spenco offices were being taken that night and we still had our props in them.

Denis and I were struggling out the door of one of them, carrying a huge sofa when Michael appeared and headed straight for us.

"Pete, Den, I just wanted to say thank you to you both for all the help you've given me throughout the film," he said.

We still had the sofa, so couldn't shake his hand, so we just said we were happy to help, it's our job, etc.

"No, I'm very grateful," he went on and pushed something into the top pockets of our shirts and walked off smiling.

Once we had put the sofa down, we inspected our pockets and found £200 in each of them.

Now, how nice was that? That had never happened to either of us or would again, so that was a pretty special moment. I waited for Leonard to do the same, but it never happened.

It was a lovely way to finish that location, and it did restore my faith a bit with the way the atmosphere had changed on the crew, and now it was back to Shepperton to finish the film.

It was the same as usual here, as you have to match up with everywhere else we had been shooting, and here we needed chickens again. Clearly, we could not get our man and his mates from the hills of St Lucia, although at the right price, I'm sure he would have come, so we found a man, not far from the studios, willing to help.

He arrived with huge crates of chicken that also included a cockerel that was making a hell of a row, so he was banned from the set and kept in a crate outside. When we had finished with them, the owner took them back to be with the cockerel, and if you have ever worked with chickens before, you'll know they can get a bit panicky at times. This was one of those occasions, and as he tried to put some chickens in with the cockerel, all hell let loose, the cockerel decided he'd had enough and made a break for freedom. He was fast and was away from the handler and into some bushes before he could be stopped.

We couldn't find him anywhere, and as the light started to go, the handler resigned himself to leaving the cockerel to fend for himself. Philosophically, he said it wouldn't last long on its own.

The following day, as we arrived at the stage in the early morning, all you could hear was this bloody cockerel doing its stuff in the undergrowth. It had survived the night, and this went on for the next three days until, on the fourth, there was silence. We never found out what happened. Did it get eaten? Did it hitch a ride back home? Did it meet a nice hen and settle down and have chicks? Who knows, but we never heard from him again.

We still had one final sequence to shoot involving a great party where the islanders have triumphed, and a band called 'The Singing Rebels' perform. This is no ordinary band, for it included such greats as Eric Clapton, George Harrison, Ringo Starr, and Ray Cooper, to name a few. All of these were on stage singing to the crew like our own personal festival, and all for free. How good is that?

As an added twist, and I mentioned this before, the name 'The Singing Rebels' used to be the band that George Harrison and his brother played in before he joined the Beatles. See, little gold nuggets everywhere!

The film had so much going for it you felt it had to be a success. It even had a Lighting Cameraman who was one of the top five in the world, Dougie Slocombe. He was unique in the way he worked as he never used a light meter but used the tone of the skin on the back of his hand to set the camera stops by, and he never got it wrong. Incredible.

It's funny, but I bumped into Dougie a few years later when I was doing commercials a lot more. I was working for a company I had done a fair bit of work for, and the PA was concerned she had picked the wrong Lighting man as he didn't have a meter. I put her mind to rest and carried on praising his abilities when he managed to fall off the set and hurt his ankle. He was taken to hospital, and the camera operator took over his duties. Yes, using a meter. Should keep my big mouth shut, really.

I don't think Dick was happy with the way the film turned out and much preferred 'Bullshot', and it wasn't a great box office success. Many reasons were banded around as to the cause of the flop. Some said Billy's character should have been played by a black actor, but the truth was, it wasn't good enough and had problems at its conception. In the beginning, Billy recalled he had gone to Heathrow to fly to St Lucia, not knowing if the money to make it was going to be raised in time. There were no mobile phones then, and it was only when he had landed that he found out that during the flight, the film was off and only as it hit the tarmac was it back on again. Seat of your pants stuff. It goes to prove you can have all the best ingredients in the world to bake a cake, but it's useless if you don't cook it properly.

Sadly, Leonard died before the film was edited, so he never saw it, and it was one of Fulton's last performances as well. Glad to have met them both, for different reasons.

While this was all going on, we were trying to get Allprops off the ground. The unit that George had found was perfect and in exactly the right location. We also had our name and all this courtesy of our 'Guv'nor'. Told you he was good, didn't I? Having finished on 'Water', there was a little time before we would go again on another film, so we all went into what amounted to an empty unit to see what we could do with it.

When it was completely empty, it looked enormous, and

the thought did cross your mind as to how we could possibly fill it. There was a small office at the front by the car park and a small kitchen and toilet down the back, and that was it. It seemed an extraordinary amount of money to pay for such basic amenities, and what with all the other bills, such as electricity, business rates, insurance, water rates, etc., you did wonder if we had done the right thing. We had no income to offset any of this, so it was all coming out of our pockets, and the fact of the matter was when we all worked, we would need someone in there to answer the phone and keep it open should we get any orders, which would be another expense.

We decided to bring anything we had at home that we didn't need or use any more and spread it out in the space, even just to make it look like a Prop Hire company. It didn't cover much of the unit when we had brought it all in, so we had to make the decision to buy stock as cheaply as we could, and from anywhere we could get it. More cash outlay.

At the end of films, the production wants to get rid of everyone as quickly as possible as it costs them money. The Prop room is generally full of bits and pieces left over from the film that was either bought or acquired in some way and hadn't got a home to go back to, like hired props. While these items are still there, the prop room stays open at a cost to production. If they can clear this and get a small reward for the stuff, they are delighted. Our plan was to use this method because we knew all the films going on, when they were finishing and who the Prop Masters were. We offered silly amounts of money to clear the prop room of anything and everything. I don't believe the Productions could believe their luck, and in a short space of time, we had acquired a vast amount of hireable stock for very little money, and the unit was starting to look the part. We got so well known for doing this that we didn't have to ask any more. Huge great trucks kept arriving without any warning, saying this is all yours if you want it, often with no money changing hands.

With so much arriving and little time to sort it out, the place was getting in a right mess, and you couldn't see what we had to hire. We needed to start putting racking and shelving up to display the items, but the cost of this was horrendous, so we had to do it a little bit at a time.

We hadn't hired a thing during this first month but had learned an awful lot about starting your own hire company. This was not going to be easy and was going to take a lot of time, energy and money, none of which was possible at the moment as George had acquired another film which, with all this expense, none of us could afford to turn down, so Allprops had to wait for a while until the wanderers returned.

We were back in Elstree Studios as our base, but this film, 'White Knights', had a number of locations, some abroad as well, so more time away from the family.

CHAPTER 23

WHITE KNIGHTS

In a dimly lit dance studio somewhere in Russia, there is a contest going on between two dancers that typifies the political conflict between East and West. As each goes through their routines, you can feel the intensity in their performances growing as they battle to come out on top, but there is a twist to this conflict. The Ballet dancer representing Russian values has defected to the West, whereas the American tap dancer has defected to the East, and neither would give an inch in making their political statements.

A haunting scene in this Taylor Hackford-directed film starring the Russian ballet dancer Mikhail Baryshnikov in the lead role and the American actor Gregory Hines as his counterpart. It also starred the well-known British actress Helen Mirren.

The story briefly is that the ballet dancer has defected to the West, but a plane heading to Japan develops engine trouble and has to put down in Russia. To hide his identity, he tries to flush all his documents down the toilet, but this is a vain attempt and doesn't fool the Russian authorities. Russia, who has an American defector of their own in Gregory, tries to use him to persuade Mikhail to return to the homeland and so make a huge international statement. Eventually, something has to give.

There is always a settling-in period at the beginning of each film when the crew and cast get to know each other and learn how each other works, and I often wondered if what I saw in people was the same as everyone else.

Denis and I were standing by again, and over a cup of tea, I said to him,

"Have you noticed that Taylor always wears a red polo shirt and green canvas trousers?"

He hadn't really noticed, so that answered my question about everyone noticing what I did.

"It can't be the same stuff every day, can it?" I mused.

"Ask him," said Den.

"That's a bit personal, isn't it?" I replied.

"Then be subtle about it," urged Den.

The ball was now firmly in my court, and as I watched him go about his work, the more I needed to know, so by chance, at another tea break, he happened to be standing next to me and catching his eye; he asked if I was ok. He was very approachable, so I went for it.

"Taylor, are they your favourite colours, red and green?"

He was way ahead of me, my subtlety being a lot less subtle than I thought it was.

"Peter," he said in his broad American accent, "you mean, why do I wear the same clothes every day, don't you?"

Now in too deep to come back, I went on, "Yes, I suppose I do."

"I have seven red polo shirts and seven pairs of green canvas trousers, all identical. I change them every day, and they get washed. The reason I do this is that while shooting, I have a million and one things to decide on, so having the same clothes means just one thing I don't have to consider."

He smiled, patted me on the shoulder, and walked off. I had to admit it did make sense when he put it like that, but I also thought that as the rest of us didn't follow this regime, did that mean we had very little on our minds other than what outfit shall I wear today?

I have mentioned call sheets before as they appear on all films, and the very first one on 'White Knights' called for the scene in the aircraft toilet where Mikhail tries to get rid of his papers, to be shot on the first day. It was a tiny set with a bit of construction work and a bit of propping to do, and shouldn't have taken long to do.

This day we were doing 'back projection' on a set where the actors stand in front of a screen that has action on it. It was taking longer than usual to do, and as the day motored on, it became clear we wouldn't get to the toilet set, so the idea was abandoned and the shot put on the following day's call sheet.

I don't know what it was about this set, but every time it was put on a call sheet, we never got round to shooting it, and this went on the entire length of the film. It became a running joke with the crew, and this set was packed up and transported to all of our locations just in case. It turned out to be the very last shot we did, and when it was over was greeted with a huge cheer from the crew.

You remember me talking about getting to know the characters of the people you worked with? One particular person really showed their true colours when we were shooting a scene in a Russian apartment. David Watkins, the Lighting Cameraman.

The Art Department had designed one wall of this apartment to be full of framed pictures; 57, to be precise. I know as I counted them. They were all glazed, all hired from Hire Companies and had a huge value to them. The shot that was devised was for the camera to track right across the set, which meant going past all of the pictures. With David's lights, the glass in the pictures was acting like a huge mirror, and the entire crew was visible. David was doing his nut and, at best, was never a happy man and was often known to disappear only to be found asleep somewhere off set. He wanted all the glass to be taken out.

We were doing this quite late at night, so time was important, and the First, Ray Corbett, a real bull of a man, wanted to know how long it would take to do this.

I explained they were all hired, and we would have to do it carefully so as not to damage any of them, so if you reckoned on a few minutes each, times 57, that would answer your question. If more people helped, you could obviously lessen that. Ray didn't like that and said he couldn't sit around with all the crew while this went on. I asked him what else he wanted us to do when a voice piped up in the background. It was David.

"Couldn't we break the glass with a hammer? It would be much quicker," he said.

I couldn't believe he had made that suggestion.

"Are you serious, David?" I shouted at him.

He did look a bit taken aback by my tone.

"What if I hit one of your lamps with a hammer? As it's quicker than turning the switch off. Would you be happy with that? Sorry, I forgot you're not happy about many things, are you?" I went on.

"I thought the First made the decisions around here, not the Prop man," he said sarcastically.

I was furious, so I went for him.

"Ok, David, we'll hit every picture with a hammer, and the production will get a bill for £10,000 from the hire companies, which you'll be happy to take out of your lighting budget, will you? Sorry, I keep mentioning happy and you in the same sentence."

He didn't say anything, shrugged his shoulders and walked off, waving a hand in the air.

It was decided to take the more cautionary approach to remove the glass, and with the help of a few people, we managed to get it done in half an hour and were now ready to shoot, but we had no Lighting man. David had gone AWOL and wasn't responding to his name being called.

"Has anyone seen David?" Ray called out in frustration.

It was now a game of 'hunt the David', and after a ten-minute search he was found asleep on a bed in another set. Unbelievable!

It was painstaking putting all the glass back in the right frames and repairing the backs so we wouldn't get charged a small fortune, but it was one of those jobs that fall at the feet of Prop Men, so we just did it and moved on. It did show how little was thought of the prop department sometimes when push came to shove.

Fortunately, we had a good relationship with the cast, who liked interacting with the crew, and for the short space of time on the film, you felt like good mates.

I particularly got on well with Gregory, who had a lot of time for everyone and was genuinely interested in you, your family, and your lives, and when possible, we had a good old chat. I was to find out how nice a man he was a little later on in the film.

We were still only shooting in the studios, but I started to feel unwell, and one morning at home, I felt so rough that I seriously could not go to work. The right side of my face felt strange, and when I looked in the mirror, I could see that the muscles weren't working properly, and it was beginning to droop. It was frightening to look at myself. I had no idea what was happening. Ann had to call George and explain, and he rejigged things and said to stay off as long as I needed to.

A panic call to the doctors and a hurriedly arranged appointment concluded that I had a condition called 'Bell's Palsy'. It is a condition that causes sudden weakness in the muscles on one side of the face when the nerve to the side of the face is squeezed by swelling and inflammation around it. It is generally temporary and improves over a few weeks in most people, but I didn't know that then, and it was frightening, to say the least. The world of Medicine doesn't know exactly what causes it, but they think it is linked to a viral infection of some sort. Apparently, a lot of Steam train drivers who used to lean out the side of their engines developed this condition with the cold winds blasting by their ears.

Once you research it, the stories that emerge from sufferers are horrendous, with some having to have their faces wired up and some never ever recovering.

You can't treat it, but I was advised to rest, keep heat to the affected part of my face and do facial exercise to get the muscles moving. For 10 days, I sat with a hot water bottle strapped to the side of my face, madly doing facial exercises, looking for the slightest glimmer of improvement. It was soul-destroying, but Ann encouraged me to keep going, and eventually I saw small improvements.

Another thing that lifted my spirits was a telephone call I received. I was sitting feeling sorry for myself when Ann said there was a 'Gregory' on the phone. She had no idea who that was, but I did. It was Gregory Hines from 'White Knights'.

He had wondered why I wasn't on set any more and went to the trouble of getting my home number and calling to see how I was doing. You don't get Hollywood stars phoning you at home very often, well, I don't anyway, so this was a bit special. We had a brief chat, which was difficult with my face the way it was, and I felt so chuffed by his concern it really did lift me. He didn't even have to bother, but he was such a nice man and went the extra mile. I really appreciated it.

After 2 weeks, I returned to the set and got a lovely reception from everyone, but one of the first people I wanted to see was Gregory to say thanks. He is, unfortunately, no longer alive, but I was pleased to have known him, if only briefly.

While I had been away, a lot of the studio shooting had been done, and the unit was off to do location shooting at RAF Machrihanish in Campbeltown in, Scotland, which was an airfield we were using to recreate the forced landing of Mikhail's plane. It was freezing with howling winds and was the last place I needed to be after just getting over Bell's Palsy, so I had an extra scarf wrapped around my head to protect myself.

With the plane being forced down, we had a large group of extras acting as Russian soldiers, and obviously they needed weapons, so we had a professional Armourer with us for safety and security reasons. The last thing you need to mislay is the odd AK47 rifle, so we had to be extremely vigilant on this location because, believe me, when mealtimes are called, extras don't care where they leave the props, as long as they get to the front of the lunch queue.

We were also shooting the plane crash landing, but as the Production couldn't afford a Boeing 747, which it would have been in real life, they used a 707 and added a lump on the forward fuselage to make it look like one. (That old trick.)

I was glad to get out of this location and off to sunnier climes, in this case, Lisbon in Portugal.

A lot of the locations picked for the film were very calculated to try and mirror the look and atmosphere of Siberia and other parts of Russia where Mikhail would have been before his defection and 'The San Carlos' theatre in Lisbon that we were going to, was no exception. It was chosen because it was the nearest one in Europe that had the same ambience and baroque elegance as the 'Kirov Theatre' in Leningrad, where Mikhail would have danced. It didn't disappoint and, in truth, was a beautiful theatre. One of the privileges you often get when working on films. It was only a short stay but well worth seeing and completing shooting; the whole unit was off to Finland, once again, to find locations similar to those of Russia.

This time we were on the island of 'Reposaari' off the Northwest coast of Finland and was selected because the light in late summer was the same unique light quality as would be in Siberia, where we couldn't film.

There was a huge amount of diplomacy involved in getting this location as the population of 1700 people were all communists and had to be convinced this film was not another 'run of the mill' anti-soviet movie. In fact, the whole area was in somewhat of an economic decline, and their port had closed, so pragmatically they thought it would bring money to the region. Not that Communist, then.

Obviously, the crew could not be housed in Reposaari, so instead, we all stayed at a hotel in a town not far away called 'Pori'. It was an unknown quantity as far as the unit was concerned, so we didn't know what to expect as we pulled up outside the hotel, but it was our home for the next three weeks, so we had to go along with it, whatever.

It was very quiet with hardly anyone around as we arrived, so it didn't look like the liveliest place to stay for any length of time, but we decided to give it a chance, have a quick shower, a drink in the bar and then go and explore the delights of 'Pori'. The bar was dead, and the crew's faces said it all, but after one drink, we all headed off in different directions from the hotel to sample the nightlife.

After hitting the town, we realised there wasn't much of a town to hit, so headed back to the hotel and were surprised to see that the street outside the hotel was a lot livelier than when we left. In fact, it was chaos, with large groups of inebriated people walking up and down the street, literally lobbing bottles across the road at each other. Not a place you would want to be, and amazingly the police were doing nothing about it other than to confine them to the pavements and let them get on with it.

It was a strange affair indeed and one I had never witnessed before or since, but we learned that this took place every Friday night, and the Police had decided to let it happen, contain it, let the drunken people let off steam, then send in a team of cleaners to clear the mess up in the morning. Everything went back to normal until next Friday. Very odd!

The night was still young, so we went for a last drink in the bar before bed, only to find that the once quiet forgotten place we had left an hour or so ago was now a heaving mass of revellers. News had got out there was a film unit in town, and everyone, it seemed, had come to look. You could hardly get in the bar, it was so packed, but the people of Pori were so nice and friendly and wanting to chat that the one drink turned into a lot more before the night was done.

It was so hot in there that I had to go outside to get some fresh air and watch the bottle fights. The air hit me and made me feel quite tired, so I decided enough was enough, and it was time for me to turn in.

As I climbed the steps of the hotel, I heard a familiar voice speak my name and looked up to see Taylor with Helen Mirren very much on his arm.

"You ok, Peter?" he said.

"Yes, thanks. I am off to bed now. What are you up to?" I said, realising that probably wasn't the best way of putting it.

They both smiled and wandered on.

I don't know if I was the first to find out or the last, but this film is where Taylor and Helen first met, fell in love and subsequently got married. I think they still are today. Don't know if my comment had anything to do with that.

Pori has fond memories and wasn't the backwater we thought it might have been when we arrived, and it was quite sad leaving it on our way to our final location in Finland; Helsinki, the Capital.

Quite different as you would expect and full of life and interesting buildings with architecture similar to Russia. The harbour, with its markets, was a lovely area, and if I'd had transport would have taken home a lot more than the small bits I did buy and could comfortably carry. I promised myself I would come back someday, I was so taken by the place, but I never did, so when we left for England, that was the last I would see of Finland.

After some final shooting back at Elstree, 'White Knights' came to an end just as 1984 was.

Like the film, 1984 was an eventful time for me, and Mr.

Orwell certainly seemed to know his stuff when he picked this year as notable.

I had started the year on a film that based itself on the book 1984, and during it had hit on the idea of starting a Prop hire company, which we had begun to do, and I had spent two weeks of my life fighting off Bell's Palsy. Two of those events were over, but Allprops was ongoing and needed all the attention we could give it. I didn't see how the present setup of us all working on films would ever work if we were to make Allprops successful, so my mind started to hatch a plan to make my time, at least, more available. I never thought that my other three partners would follow suit, and as it turned out, they never did, but my thoughts were different from theirs, and I had to do what best suited me and my family.

I didn't know at the time, but White Knights would be the last full film I ever worked on, but right now, it was time to go home and spend Christmas with my family and have a well-earned rest before taking 1985 by the horns. It was certainly lovely being home, and the girls, being 7 and 4 now, were old enough to really appreciate what Christmas was all about. It was these times that I wanted more of before they grew too old, and being in Allprops full time would give me the opportunity to do this; I just had to engineer a way of doing this and still be able to pay the bills.

I had worked a lot in 1984 and just as well with Allprops being another pull on our finances, so I wasn't in too bad a financial position as 1985 started, but it's amazing how quickly your money dwindles when you stop working, so I had to 'toe the line' until I could change things.

None of us had anything lined up immediately after Xmas, so we all spent time in Allprops, putting racks up and generally sorting things out. It was then that Allprops made a breakthrough. A phone call asking if we had a period tape recorder that worked had the four of us scrambling around, trying to get one of the ones we had acquired to perform. We had already said yes, and a van was on its way to pick it up, so this was something that had to happen. With parts from the other ones all over the floor, we managed to get one going just before the van arrived. Our first order. Not a big one, I know, but we had started, and now the only way was up.

I was enjoying being here so much, I could quite easily have stopped doing films there and then if I could have, but financially it wasn't viable yet, and when Les asked me to do a few weeks on a film he had just been offered, I couldn't say no. I wasn't standing by this time, just helping out with dressing, so it was strange being off the set for the first time in a very long time, but I was earning, and that was enough. What it also meant was that two of the partners would be absent from Allprops for a while when they were most needed.

CHAPTER 24

LINK

As the camera looms up over a rustic brick wall at the side of a Scottish field, we reveal a whole flock of sheep slaughtered, covered in their own blood, and we see the rear end of a car departing with the face of a chimpanzee peering out of the back window. We are led to believe there is a connection here and that somehow everyone has been duped. The answer is never given as this is the final shot in the horror movie 'Link', a 1985 film directed by the Australian, Richard Franklin.

Terence Stamp is the main actor playing an eccentric professor doing experiments with Chimpanzees to find the link between humans and monkeys. He has three living at his house, one of which dresses as a butler and performs butler's duties. The professor takes on an assistant, played by the American actress Elisabeth Shue, who, when the professor mysteriously disappears, finds herself fighting an increasingly aggressive Chimpanzee called Link, with the resulting mayhem.

The Chimpanzee used was, in fact, an Orangutan whose fur was dyed and who wore prosthetic ears to more resemble a chimp, and was trained by the highly renowned animal trainer Ray Berwick, together with a team of very able-bodied assistants. They were brilliant with Link, and watching while they performed was amazing and often very funny.

Richard was also the producer and had previous films under his belt, including 'Psycho 2'. He never looked the part to me and reminded me more of a banker than a director and seemed devoid of any personality, but I might have missed something as he was very successful at what he did, but he also hid a secret.

He had a crush on Elisabeth, and it was obvious to anyone who watched him when he was around her, like a fawning schoolboy in love with a girl who is way out of his league. The one problem with all of this was that Elisabeth wasn't in the least bit interested in his advances, and that showed as well, so there were a few awkward moments during filming.

Once we had dressed the main sets in Shepperton, Les sent me with a dressing crew to our locations in St Abbs in Scotland, just on the Scottish borders, and we were put in a pub in a small coastal town called Eyemouth, 8 miles north of Berwick-upon-Tweed.

It was a family-run pub, and they looked after us very well, being more than happy to have all their rooms booked up for three weeks by a free-spending film crew. It didn't take long for word to get round about our arrival, and soon their bar was packed out with inquisitive folk interested in the goings on. The pub landlord was even happier with a full bar as his takings shot up so much that he had to put in an extra order with the brewery.

This had all the markings of an easy ride, but future events were to change all of that and make this location one to forget.

Most of the dressing we had to do in Scotland was straightforward, but the location which was causing us so many problems was the last shot of the film, where all the slaughtered sheep are revealed. There wasn't a lot of dressing to do other than get a quantity of already dead sheep scattered around the field and covered in fake blood.

To obtain the sheep, we had approached a local abattoir to see if they had enough sheep that had died from natural causes for us to use in this scene and were surprised when they said yes. All we had to do was go and pick them up, but they did warn us that they were not in great condition.

So, with 2 drivers and their tip-up flatback trucks, 3 other Prop men and myself, we went on the designated day to collect the sheep. Once on the trucks, we felt we could just tip the back up and push them off where we needed them instead of manhandling each one. It was a good plan, or so we thought.

Greeted by the manager of the abattoir, we backed our trucks up to the doors of the sheds where the sheep were, and he pulled open the doors. The force of the smell inside hit us full-on. It was like something you can't describe, and believe me you would not want to experience this. The air was so thick with the stench you felt as if you were physically penetrating it as you entered, and it might not have been so bad if we all hadn't gone 'on the lash' the night before in the pub, which seemed to have no 'drinking up time' at all. We had all drunk far too much and were now beginning to regret that decision, big time.

Nevertheless, this had to be done, so I pulled my scarf over my nose, braced myself and entered the shed. As I looked behind me, I saw that I was on my own. Two of the other Prop Men, who weren't feeling great when we left the pub in the morning, were now in an even worse state, and one was being physically sick, with the other not far off. They were refusing to go in, and the two drivers were only there to drive, so our party was reduced to me, one other Prop and the manager, who was used to all this and found it rather amusing.

With some large protective gloves, we set about getting the carcasses out of this pungent abyss and onto the trucks. The state of the sheep was worse than I could possibly have imagined, and each one took the three of us to load, and there were 20 of them. Every so often, we had to leave the sheds to get air, take stock and force ourselves back in, but eventually, after what seemed like an eternity, we had them all loaded.

Getting them off at the other end worked well, and with the open trucks, the smell had dissipated a lot. With the Art Department, we dressed them around the field, covered them in fake blood and waited for the unit to arrive, which was in about half an hour.

I looked down at my clothes. They were in a terrible state and stank to high heaven of rotting sheep, and I couldn't get their smell out of my nostrils. No amount of washing my hands and face and blowing my nose would make a difference, but I had to go through the procedure in reverse when we returned the sheep, and this time they would be covered in blood, so I just put up with it.

The main unit arrived, and Richard, the First and the Lighting Cameraman, came to view the set. Richard was happy, and so was the First. The third member of the trio had been looking up at the sky and was not so happy.

He took the other two to one side, and Richard's happy face took on a different expression. This was the final shot of the film and had to be shot in brilliant sunlight, which we clearly did not have, and the forecasts said we wouldn't have for the rest of our stay in Scotland. Everyone who mattered seemed to form a huddle in the middle of the field, but nothing was going to change the fact that we couldn't shoot this today, so all our efforts had been in vain.

With the weather forecasts the way they were, we wouldn't shoot this shot at this location. The word beginning with B and ending with ks came from my lips.

We went slowly around the field and collected all the sheep and drove back to the abattoir where we met the manager, who could hardly contain himself when we told him. We thanked him, said we wouldn't need them again due to the weather being so bad, tipped the sheep out and left in our dirty stinking clothes to try and clean up at the hotel.

I didn't feel I could touch anything and was aching to get in a shower and stay there for four months, and at the hotel I did spend a very long time washing, but it seemed to make no difference. The smell had penetrated my every pore and would only leave when it was ready.

Fortunately, we had the weekend off and decided we should see a bit more of Scotland while we had the chance, and with Edinburgh not too far away, we planned a tour of the city on Sunday.

Unfortunately, we had to negotiate a Saturday night in a pub bar before our trip, and what started out as a quiet night turned into an unfettered drinking session with thoughts of the following day's excursion being totally forgotten.

Rounding up the now very unwilling 'tourists' in the morning proved difficult, and the enthusiasm was definitely waning. All the car windows were down as the two Prop men who had performed so woefully at the abattoir were sitting in the back of the car, and we weren't going to take any chances.

It seemed to take longer than we thought it would, and there was a growing feeling of 'let's just go home' when we finally arrived at our destination just around lunchtime. I don't think food was on anyone's mind, but I personally wanted a drink, having done all the driving. Whether we had come to the wrong city, I don't know, but everything seemed shut. Does Edinburgh shut on a Sunday? It felt less than inviting after our epic journey, and after a quick drive around, the consensus of opinion was that this was a mistake and we should drive back. Life on the edge!

Then I saw a department store that had a café, so I pulled over. It wasn't the nicest, but they did tea and other bits, so we decided to give it a try. Our delicately stomached Prop man chose a milky flavoured drink to 'line his stomach', he said, but unfortunately, on the way back we saw that drink disappear out of the car window.

Arriving back at Eyemouth, rather less than satisfied with our day out, we all dispersed to our respective rooms to fine-tune our bodies for tomorrow's rigours, although we did have a few drinks in the bar that night just to be sociable.

The days went by until it was time for us to leave and go home, and the night before our departure, our landlord and his family laid on 'a bit of a do' to say goodbye and thank you. Les had already recalled two of the Prop Men back to Shepperton, so there was only me, one other Prop and a driver, which shouldn't have mattered until halfway through the evening I got a call from Production.

They had checked the weather, had discussions and decided that they now wanted to shoot the final scene with the sheep again and asked if I could check if the sheep were still available.

I put the phone down, hardly believing what I had just heard. Were they serious? It was bad enough the first time, but now we were three, including the driver and the other Prop with me was the one who was physically sick the first time and would have been as much use as a chocolate teapot. I had just felt like the stench was leaving me, and now the nightmare was reoccurring. This was going to be the manager and me on our own again; I could see it coming.

It was around 9pm when I made the call, not expecting anyone to pick up on a Saturday night, but he was there. (Get a life, for God's sake!) Amazingly, the same sheep were there as we had left them, but over the last couple of weeks had really started to deteriorate.

I called the Production half thinking should I lie and tell them he didn't have any, but I thought better of it and told the truth, like a fool.

Considering what we were facing the following day, I decided to cut back on the beer consumption that night, and the other Prop was given a 'yellow card' warning, but remembering what he experienced before, he wasn't hard to convince, and our last night of celebrations turned into an early night.

At 6.30am the next morning, when we should have been having our farewell breakfast, followed by a leisurely drive home, we headed off to the abattoir, and the conversation in the truck was decidedly muted.

As we entered the car park, we were greeted by our smiling manager. He was loving this.

"Are you sure you want these sheep? They are in a bad way now," he mocked.

I really didn't, but had a job to do.

"Yep. We need to get this shot, and the weather today is apparently perfect for it," I said.

"Well, they are in the shed waiting for you," he smirked.

His smile was definitely getting broader as he recognised the other Prop from before.

"Are you ok going in? The smell is worse."

No words were necessary, as his look spoke volumes.

"We can't put this off any longer. Can you open the doors for us, and we'll back the truck in." I said reluctantly.

As he opened them up, the smell was horrendous, physically pushing you back. Up went the scarves, off went my mate being sick again, and he wasn't ever going to go in that shed. My driver was of no use either, so I turned to the manager.

"Looks like you and me again."

He laughed out loud and entered. I wasn't sure I was up to this either, but our options were limited, so I forced myself inside. He hadn't lied. The sheep were in one hell of a state and should not have been making this journey. There was gunge coming out of every orifice, and I seriously did not want to touch them, but me and our man dragged these disgusting sheep's bodies onto the truck, and when we finished, my 'new' work clothes were as bad as the first one's I had thrown away. This was becoming an expensive hobby.

We were finally loaded. My mate had controlled his stomach movements, and we had stopped the manager laughing as we pulled out of the abattoir with our smelly cargo.

A quick rerun of our previous dressing, and all was ready again for the unit. Richard was pleased, the First was pleased, and so was the Lighting Cameraman, so we shot it. As the unit left the field, we surveyed our final task. Another round of 'tote the smelly sheep'. This time would be the last time we touched them, for when we got to the abattoir, all we had to do was push the button and tip them off.

As we arrived, the manager was smiling. (Had he even stopped?)

"I'll open up, and you can tip them off," he said

The driver backed in and hit the button. We waited, but nothing happened.

"Have you pushed the button?" I shouted.

"I'm pushing it now. Nothing is happening," he shouted back.

"For F***s sake. Let me have a go," I roared.

I lost count of the number of times I pushed, but nothing happened.

Our manager was in tears as I slowly got out of the cab. We all knew what this meant. My mate was off, and the driver stayed in the cab.

Out of sheer anger and frustration, I hurled the sheep off the truck. (Sorry, ladies!) My clothes were ruined again, and the smell clung to me once more. I felt wretched.

Back at the room in the pub, I bagged up my clothes for humane disposal and once again sat in a hot shower for an awfully long time, with the same results as before. I still felt grubby, and I couldn't get the smell out of my nostrils.

We did have a lot of drinks that night, celebrating the fact that we wouldn't have to see those bloody sheep again.

We finished at Shepperton and cleared the Prop room. We also did our tried and tested trick and offered the production money to clear the prop room, which they were more than happy to take, and Allprops had some more stock. With Les as Prop master, we had also been able to hire some of our stuff to the film, so all in all it had been good for us. The film itself didn't fare so well, and any idea of 'Link 2' was soon shelved.

It was now home and a bit of a rest before going in and carrying the work on at Allprops. I hadn't mentally decided this, but Link would be the last film I worked on for another 6 years, and then only to help Les out. In our absence, Allprops had started to get more orders and needed someone in there full time, so we had employed Denis's Dad, Len, who was retired, to come in each day and man the phone. He obviously was an elderly man and had physical limitations to what he could do, but he was very willing, and for a while we coped. As Allprops began to get known, the workload had increased and was beginning to get too much for him, and clearly Denis was worried about his old dad, as you would be.

Len decided to call it a day, and Denis found a replacement for him in the form of an old drinking partner at his local who was nearly as old as Len. Not a huge step forward, but beggars can't be choosers, and 'Arthur' joined the ranks.

He had a sort of swagger to his walk like a drunken waiter and considered himself a bit of a charmer with the ladies. More in his head, I think. I don't think he had realised what he had let himself in for, and soon the swagger turned into frenzied running as he tried to cope with orders, answering the phone, etc.

After returning from Link and witnessing this, my mind was made up. We couldn't go on like this and be successful. One of us at least had to be in there full time, and I realised the obvious person to do that was me. We couldn't expect two pensioners to make our business a world-beater, and that's not what I envisaged when conceiving the idea with Denis. I couldn't do film work due to the amount of time spent away, Allprops couldn't afford to pay me a big enough wage, so the only means open to me was to move over into another form of film work; doing Commercials, which paid better money for less time, but they were hectic, and you were generally on your own taking all the flack. It had to be done.

CHAPTER 25

MY NEW CAREER

It wasn't that I wanted to do commercials; I just didn't see how else I could go forward. I hadn't done many, didn't really enjoy doing them and had virtually no contacts on that side of things that would get me constant work, so this, in a way, was like going back to 1978 and starting again.

As I have said, I still had the usual household bills to cover and was now supporting our company's progress, so it wasn't the odd one here and there I had to find; it was a continuous flow of them, and who was going to provide me with that?

There had been several agencies popping up acting as the go-between for commercial companies and crew, but I had no idea which one was the best for me until a chance encounter with an Art Department 'Stylist' at Allprops changed all that.

I had been there a while after finishing 'Link' and was really enjoying being in the thick of it. If it wasn't for the financial side of things, I couldn't have been happier, and I was home every night to see Ann and the girls, which is what I wanted for my life.

While doing some paperwork in the office, the door opened

and in walked the 'Stylist'. Her name was Belinda, and she had heard about our company and wanted to have a look round. At this point, there was something more substantial to look round, so I gave her the guided tour, and she seemed impressed and hired a few items.

In the office, having tea, we got to talking about what she did and how she got started, and she told me she used one of the Agencies, and it worked well for her. She also said she thought it was a good one for me and that I should give them a call and talk it over. We got on well, and I decided to take her advice.

That night I went home and discussed it with Ann, and we agreed it was a good idea, so the following day, I phoned them and got all the details about pay, their fees, etc. Belinda had also forewarned them I might call and had put a good word in for me, which was unexpected but nice.

I had to do the maths and work out with my overheads, how many days I would need to do to be able to live and how many days more it would give me to be at Allprops. It seemed to work, so I bit the bullet and signed up with them, which meant another monthly outgoing for their fees and, until work came in, added more pressure on our finances.

This was a difficult time for us as a family. Ann could see what I was trying to do, but it did put pressure on us all. I was trying to build a better life for us and to have more time to be part of that life, but that meant taking a few risks, Allprops being one of those. I wasn't infallible and made mistakes like everyone else. This investment could have been a massive financial misjudgement, but in my mind, I knew I had to make it work, and if there was one thing I had learned on films, it was that you didn't give up when there was a job to be done.

Right now, the company was moving in the right direction, and the four of us were dragging in orders from wherever we could. Any money we made went straight back into more racking and better facilities, and soon it started to look and feel like a proper Hire Company.

I was immersed in it all when the phone rang. It was the Agency, and they wanted to confirm a three-day soup commercial with me starting the very next day. There was only one answer to that, so I went home early to prepare my equipment and maybe nick a few things from our kitchen I thought I might need for soup. The world I was entering would require a whole new range of equipment to the type I used on films, and with the vast number of different products to deal with, you never finished buying new stuff to deal with all the problems you encountered.

It was a lonely experience doing my first commercial after propping on films for so long. There was no one to ask, and all the decisions were yours, ones that you lived or died from, and the companies you worked for had very little loyalty to you if they needed a scapegoat.

I got through the soup commercial relatively unscathed (another one in the can), and the production company said they were pleased and would look forward to working with me in the future. I learned that was commercial talk for if we can't get our usual Prop Man, we might use you again.

The truth of the matter was that commercials were a means to an end and something I had to do, whether I liked them or not. They weren't so dissimilar to feature films, just a lot smaller, but the emphasis was on the product and making it look wonderful, although some did use a storyline to promote their ideas. As I got more involved, I made a lot of good friends and contacts and began to get more and more work, sometimes more than I wanted. They helped me keep my head above water financially and gave me the time to develop our company, and this was how 1985 was to pan out for me, with a combination of Allprops and commercials filling my weeks.

At Christmas, we were able to plan exactly what we wanted to do rather than muddle something together around my workload, and we didn't know it, but it would be the last one we spent in this house, for Ann had been looking around the local area for another house so we could get more garden for the girls to play in; and more living space for us all.

We had made the decision for Ellie to go to a local private school, and at the right age, Ria would follow in her footsteps, so with that in mind, we concentrated on an area nearer their school and put out the feelers to Estate Agents in the area. I really didn't have a lot of spare time, so Ann took all of this on and began to build up a list of properties to view. Many you could easily discount either because of price, location or facilities, so the list wasn't very long and not very exciting, if I'm honest. We got a bit disheartened with the lack of choice, and the idea cooled for a few weeks until one evening, I arrived home after being at Allprops to be greeted with,

"Don't take your coat off. We are viewing a property in half an hour."

It was a few miles from where we lived, but in a much nicer area, which was reflected in the price and ideal for the girl's school. It was a lovely, detached house with a large back garden with 4 huge oak trees overlooking a field where horses grazed, a big front garden and driveway and two more bedrooms. Pretty much all of the features we were looking for.

I think we knew we wanted it 5 minutes after we arrived, but there were still a few obstacles to overcome, and we hadn't put our house on the market yet. The couple selling it was going through a divorce and wanted to sell quickly, so were open to doing a deal, but there was still a large gap between their price and what we could get for ours. It would mean us getting a bigger mortgage, which would be based on my previous earnings, and it wasn't a certainty, with my chopping and changing my work around from films to commercials, that they would be enough.

I could see Ann really wanted it, and I agreed it would be a good move for us all, so we agreed a price based upon us selling ours, and soon we were on the market with all our fingers crossed.

As I have said before, fate was waiting round the corner and presented us with a lady who wanted to move in quickly, which suited us all. The funny thing was the new kitchen we had decided was necessary, was the one thing the lady said she wanted to change. Can't please everyone, obviously. We negotiated a new mortgage, and within a few months we were in, making plans to turn this into our forever home.

The extra money needed for everything meant I had to step up my commercial work, if I could, at the expense of time in Allprops, which was a bit counter to what I had intended, but life, as we all find out, isn't always the way you want it to be no matter how many plans you make.

No matter, we all loved the new house, and it was to be ours for quite a few years and bring some lovely memories, including the birth of our son Harry in 1989.

Over the years, I did hundreds of commercials, and the frequency of them often made them blend into each other. I have forgotten more than I can remember, but the few I mention in this book will give you a flavour of what they were like. They had the same format as feature films, but were smaller scale and ran like a parallel universe.

CHAPTER 26

COMMERCIALS

As I think about the commercials I did, so many stories come to mind and probably would make up a book on their own, but I couldn't leave this side of my career without mentioning one more which took me to the other side of the world. It was with a company that I did a huge amount of work for and who treated the crew extremely well, in stark contrast to, say, Quentin. They wanted everyone to be happy and went out of their way to make sure it happened. The producer, Roger, was a gay man but was so nice and was the instigator of all that was good about Brian Byfield Films, and it was he who booked me on this 'Ryvita' commercial that was being shot in the Maldives, somewhere I had never been. I was so looking forward to this, but as was usual with overseas locations, you had to trim your equipment down to a bare minimum as the cost of transporting it that distance was horrendous.

The budget was tight, and so Roger had asked if some of us could double up as departments to save on crew costs. I was asked if I could do construction as well as props, makeup to do hairdressing as well, and so on.

There wasn't much construction on this, so I readily agreed, not wanting to miss out. I really did have to trim the cloth if I was going to take construction bits as well, so I left on the plane with the distinct feeling that I didn't have all I might need.

It was a long journey via Dubai, then Colombo in Sri Lanka, with a half-day stay because of connecting flights and finally to the capital of the Maldives, Male.

At Colombo, we were met in a highly decorated Sri Lankan bus overly draped in beads and religious paraphernalia, which we thought was our personal transport to the hotel, but the driver had other ideas. Once we were all aboard, the driver took off like a bat out of hell, blasting his horn continually and swerving in and out of traffic like a maniac. I've never seen so many frightened faces on one bus, and everyone was clinging on for dear life. Then all of a sudden, he slammed the brakes on and skidded to a halt, opening the folding door as he did so.

On got another Sri Lankan man who just smiled and sat down as if this were a normal occurrence. He said nothing for the rest of the journey to the hotel, where he just got off the bus and wandered off. Bizarre!

We found out later it was the driver's cousin, and as he was in the area, offered to pick him up and give him a lift to the hotel. Why not?

After a half day rest in rooms allocated at the hotel, we got the connecting flight to Male, where we boarded some small trucks for a short journey to the harbour. There we offloaded everything on to some small boats to take us across to the island we were shooting on.

As we stepped off the boat, I looked at my watch. We had been travelling for the best part of 36 hours without a lot of rest, and everyone was exhausted, but as you looked at the turquoise water surrounding the white sandy beached island, you had to say it was worth it just to see this.

Union rules meant, however, that after a journey like that,

you had to have the next day off to recuperate, and how I was looking forward to that; but for now, it was food and bed. All the rooms overlooked the Ocean, for the island was tiny and only took about 10 minutes to walk round, and the gentle lapping of the waves soon had me in a deep slumber.

However, the heat in the morning made it impossible to lie in, so after breakfast, I decided to find a nice shady area and catch up on my sleep. In the perfect spot, my eyelids started to feel very heavy, and I was drifting off when I heard my voice being called. It was Roger in a panic. Should I ignore it and pretend I hadn't heard him? But then it wouldn't take long for him to find me with the size of the island, so I shouted back.

"Thank God. There's been a catastrophe with the picket fence that was made in Male, and Brian wants you to redo it," he explained.

I didn't even know we had a picket fence in this.

"Have you got an electric sander?" he said.

Was he serious? When I was trimming my equipment down to the bare bones, bringing my electric sander halfway across the world to a country with a different electrical voltage than in the UK, making it entirely useless, didn't feature heavily in my plans. It wouldn't normally have been my problem, but as I was now construction as well, it had become mine.

I politely said I didn't, but could I look at the fence to see its condition? It was a bloody mess and had been coated in a strange texture that I couldn't put my finger on and would need stripping right back and starting again.

As the fence sat behind the main artist, it was vital that it was right for tomorrow. My day off just walked out the door. I didn't have the right tools for this, and even the bit of sandpaper and a wire brush Roger had bought to help wasn't going to cut the mustard, so I had to find something else. This was an example of the type of problem a Prop Man is continually handed to sort out with no warning or time to work with, so I wasn't surprised by my dilemma.

I reasoned the hotel must have a maintenance department and might have tools I could borrow, so I went to the reception, and they sent me round the back of the building to the workshops. None of the workers spoke English, and my Sri Lankan was non-existent, so trying to explain what I wanted was like a game of Charades with arm gestures. I think I was getting through to them when, fortunately, in came another worker who did speak English. As I explained again, his eyes lit up, and he went over to a big wooden chest in the corner and emerged with an electric wire brush. It wasn't exactly what I had intended, but it was all he had and was very pleased to lend it to me. How could I refuse? I thanked him and went to leave the workshop and found he was coming with me. Whether he had designated himself my First Lieutenant or he just didn't want to let his power tool out of his sight, I don't know, but he was going to be with me until the bitter end.

We got to the jetty where the fence was, and I asked him where we could get an electrical supply for the brush. He smiled and scraped the sand away from beneath him to reveal a plug socket in the sand by the side of the jetty.

Obviously, I let him plug it in and, recognising he was still alive, started the brush and laid into the fence. It was certainly doing its job, and loads of stuff was flying off, but my assistant was laughing.

"What?" I said.

He pointed at me, so I looked down at my clothing, and it was as if I had been covered in a spider's web, and I then realised why the fence texture looked strange. It had been painted in enamel paint, which is very thick, strong and totally unsuitable for wood, and the brush had been spinning it into a thread that made me look as if I were in a cocoon.

It took the two of us the rest of the day to sort this mess out, and barring a short visit from Roger with a sandwich and a beer, we never saw any of the rest of the crew, who were probably enjoying their day off as I should have been.

With Roger's nod of approval after finishing, we headed back to the hotel. My mate had been fantastic, so I gave him a bundle of local currency for his help, which he was over the moon about. Probably more than he earned in a month, but his help was invaluable.

All I wanted now was a shower, some food, some drink and some sleep; in that order. It was nice to sit down and finally relax, for tomorrow we would be out in the roasting sun trying to sell crispy biscuits. It did seem a surreal thing to do, travelling all this way to encourage the sale of Ryvita's, but thank you very much to the person who came up with the idea and pushed it through.

I did get a bit of free time and tried snorkelling, which was a fantastic experience, but managed to badly burn my back in the sun as I forgot to wear a tee-shirt, and the journey back home was quite uncomfortable. Nevertheless, I wouldn't have missed this trip, whatever the drawbacks to it, as it was a wonderful place to visit, and I told Ellie and Ria all about it. Some years later, when Ellie got married, she and her husband Ian went there for their honeymoon. I don't know if I had influenced her, but she loved it as well.

I worked for Brian Byfield Films on many occasions, and they took me to many other foreign locations, and we were always so well looked after. It was a sad time for me when I finally gave up doing commercials and stopped working for them. I had made so many friends there, but I think their setup was changing anyway, so probably good timing in hindsight.

The stories that came out of working on commercials were equally as bizarre and funny as those on films, but I did so many of them, as I said, so I couldn't possibly include them all in this book. Maybe if I write another book, but who knows?

We arrived back in England, and after a short spell at home growing the skin again on my back, I ventured back into Allprops to do another stint.

Although I had made the transition to commercials, I occasionally did bits on films, as I was still getting calls from Prop

Masters that I had worked with, but never a full film again.

On one of those occasions, I got a call to do a few days on a film that was shooting at Shepperton, but was going out to Spain as well. I can't remember the name of it, but no matter. My job was purely to strike a set and return the props, so I went on stage and realised there was a lot to do and probably needed someone else to help. One of the reasons I had got a call was that the film industry at this time was so busy it was difficult getting crew, so they had enticed me out of semi-retirement to help them. Getting another person would be difficult, but the Prop Master said to phone the Union and see who was on the books. There weren't many, obviously, so I took the first name and asked them to turn up at Shepperton the following day.

I hadn't worked with this Prop Man before, so I didn't know what to expect, but the next day, Michael turned up at the Prop room. He was no spring chicken, had a very broad Irish accent, which made it difficult to understand him, and wore the thickest pair of glasses I had ever seen on anyone. They were almost like a joke pair. Could he see through them at all?

He was very pleasant, so after a cup of tea and a bit of a chat, Michael and I went off to the stage to carry on striking.

"What will you have me doing?" he asked.

"If you move all the items I've already ticked off on that table to these empty tables, we'll pack them up," I replied.

He thought about it for a second, then picked up an empty cardboard box and proceeded to fill it. Once he was satisfied he had enough, he picked it up, walked over to the empty table and managed to completely miss the end of it, dropping the box and its entire contents on the stage floor. I can still hear the sound of those items smashing.

"What the f**k are you doing?" I shouted. "That'll cost us hundreds of pounds in damages."

"I'm so sorry. I missed the edge of the table," he tried to explain.

Did he even see the table?

"Why didn't you put the box in the middle? The table is empty," I shouted.

"I thought I'd start at this end," he went on.

There was no answer to that.

"I'd better go and try and explain this to the Prop Master. Just stay here and don't touch anything else until I get back."

"Yes, sir. I will do that," he replied and sat down.

He'd only been on stage 10 minutes and had already become a liability. I didn't know if I could trust him with the props, so after a chat with the Prop Master, we decided he should just sit in the Prop room and man the phone, as the Prop master had to pop out for a short while.

There was a Lighting Hire company van arriving that day to deliver two huge glass chandeliers, which were being shipped out to Spain for shooting, so Michael was just to jot down the time they were being delivered when the Company called in. As he sat there, the phone rang. The Lighting Company was already at Shepperton and was coming round to the Prop room. Michael, in the absence of the Prop Master, was in charge and so opened the doors and the huge lights were carefully brought in.

It had all gone ok up to this point until it was explained that the chandeliers came in sections for transportation, and they had to show someone how it was done. Well, there was only Michael, so for half an hour, they took him through every detail before they left.

A few minutes after their departure, the Prop Master returned to be confronted by the huge wooden crates holding the lights.

"When did they arrive?" he said to Michael.

"Half an hour or so ago," replied Michael.

"But they were supposed to let me know when they were coming so they could show me how to assemble them," he said.

"That's ok, they have shown me," Michael said proudly.

"They showed you?" the Prop Master said disbelievingly.

"Yes, they did," smiled Michael.

"So, you are the only one who knows how these bloody things go together, and you're not even on the film. Christ, why didn't they wait for me? Now we are right in the shit."

Originally, the Prop Master was to be shown as he was going out to Spain, but fate had conspired to alter that scenario and place that responsibility squarely in the hands of an elderly Irishman with failing eyesight, who was next to useless and not even on the film.

After desperate attempts to get the Lighting Company back to show him, which failed, it was decided that Michael had to go out to Spain as the chandelier expert, as the lights were being shipped out that night, so there was no alternative.

That's what happened, and Michael got two weeks paid employment in Spain as the 'expert' when he was only supposed to have been coming in for one day's work to help strike a set, where his only contribution was to smash a box full of hired props.

Rumour has it that when called upon to assemble the chandeliers, he had no idea at all, and they had to get a Spanish expert in to help them. Isn't life wonderful sometimes?

CHAPTER 27

BEST INTENTIONS

I had managed to balance commercials and Allprops well so far and make enough money to pay the bills in our new house, which we had been in for about a year now, and we had started to make changes to make it more ours.

It was a large area of garden to look after, and with my time limitations and Ann's commitments with the girls' schooling and looking after the house, we decided to get help with it, employing an Italian gardener called George.

He was so knowledgeable and began to treat it as if it was his, bringing in plants he had cultivated at home to enhance 'his' garden. We didn't mind, he was saving us a fortune in plants, and the garden was starting to transform into a beautiful space.

He had also convinced us that getting a greenhouse would open up so many other possibilities for 'growing on' cuttings, etc., so when I saw an advert in the local paper for a greenhouse that the owner didn't want and was free to whoever would take it away, I jumped at it.

With the help of George and his gardener's vehicle, we took

it apart and somehow got it back in one piece. Unfortunately, I didn't get round to putting it together until late in the year, bringing plenty of sarcastic comments from George.

Finally, halfway through October 1987, I built a base, assembled the frame, and carefully put all the glass in. I had put it next to a wooden shed we had bought, and together it made it look as if we knew what we were doing.

I stood back and admired my handy work, being very pleased I had finished it as I was starting a commercial in Pinewood studios the next day.

I watched the news that night, and the weatherman at that time, Michael Fish, had spurned any idea of there being a storm that night, as some people had predicted.

During the night of the 15th of October 1987, there was one of the worst storms this country had experienced in many, many years. Winds were at record speeds, and so many trees came down, blocking roads all over England. I awoke thinking how quiet it was, as normally there would have been road traffic noise outside, but there was none.

As I looked out the back window, there was devastation. A huge 15-metre bough had broken off one of our large Oak trees and crashed onto the newly erected greenhouse, smashing it to pieces, then rolled over and embedded itself in the lawn. We'd had our new greenhouse up for just one day, and now it was a pile of twisted metal and broken glass. I can't tell you how I felt looking at it, but I couldn't do anything but leave it as I had to drive to Pinewood, so I jumped in my car and headed off down the road.

I got 200 metres down the road and had to stop. There was a huge tree that had come down, blocking the road, but I managed to ease around it, only to be confronted by another one a little further on. I could see there were loads of these all down the road, so I turned around and headed back, choosing to find another route, but going back the other way proved to be just the same. It was blocked by trees as well, which is why it had been so quiet. No one could go anywhere, and that included me, and I was supposed to be going to Pinewood to do a job.

As I have said before, generally there is only one Prop on commercials, and this was the case with this one, but there was no way I could get there. I had never not turned up before, apart from when Ellie was born and I didn't want to repeat the failure, but I couldn't think of a way out of it. Then I began to think that if I was having trouble, then maybe everyone was; hardly anyone would be able to get there, and they may well postpone it.

I got back to the house to find Ann and the girls looking out the back window at the state of our garden, and they wondered why I was back so quickly until I explained about the roads. Some fencing had come down as well, and it looked like a disaster zone. The one good thing from Ellie and Ria's point of view was they would be having a day off school, as we couldn't get them there.

I called the Production company at Pinewood to let them know what had happened, expecting them to say it was ok, loads hadn't made it in, but they didn't. I was the only one not in, and I truly believe they thought I was lying and was making an excuse not to be there. We never worked together again, which only goes to prove what I said about the company's loyalties in the commercial world.

I felt awful letting them down. This just was not me, but I wasn't sure what else I could have done, so I put the phone down, feeling rather deflated. Not my finest hour. Only a small thing, I know, but it has stayed in my mind all this time.

One thing was for sure; this wouldn't be a day off with the work awaiting me in the back garden. The greenhouse was a complete write-off; I had to dig down into the lawn and cut off as much of the branch as I could before filling it back in and levelling the lawn. Would have preferred going to Pinewood.

As for Mr. Fish, that statement has haunted him ever since

and is often brought up on television prior to other big storms coming our way.

It goes to prove you can have the best intentions in the world, but sometimes you have no control over what happens.

There were many stories to come out of that house over the years, and maybe one day I'll do them justice and put them into print, but for now, I'll finish off what was left of my film career.

CHAPTER 28

THE END OF FILMS

Apart from the odd days here and there to help out old mates on films, I didn't do anything but commercials and try to push Allprops forward until 1991, when I got a call from a Production Designer called John Beard, who was picking up the last few weeks of a French-made film that was coming to London on location and he wanted me as a standby.

It was actually a nice change from doing commercials, as they can become a bit full on, and this was a nice change of pace.

It was called "Map of the Human Heart" and starred a lot of French actors I had never heard of. Not that it mattered, but I never really got to know any of them, or them me.

It was straightforward stuff in and around London, but it did take us inside the Albert Hall and on to the roof, where you could see right down inside the Hall. A magnificent view, although I never liked heights.

The one memorable thing for me on this was they gave me a credit as a standby prop. When I think of all the other films I had done where I got no credit at all, this did seem bizarre, but I'll take it. I was obviously meant to come out of retirement again.

There was one more film in my locker before I would finally call it a day, but before that, I wanted to mention a few weeks I did on a film a few years back with the Director, Michael Winner, who did three 'Death Wish' films as well as a host of others. If not only to illustrate the different ways Directors go about their business, but he did also deliver such a great line on set one day that it would be remiss of me not to include it.

Overall, on films, as I said, I only worked with the same director on two occasions. Jim Henson on the two Muppet films and Dick Clement on the two HandMade films. Both of those were really calm, polite, and very approachable, and that made the crew and cast feel completely at ease. Michael Mann on 'The Keep', was different in that he had absolute control and tolerated no one's opinion but his own. Taylor Hackford was a real gentleman and gained respect, as he respected everyone else's contribution.

All Directors have their way own way of doing things to achieve the final product, so when I got a call to do a week on a film called 'The Wicked Lady' directed by Michael Winner, I was a bit concerned as he had a terrible reputation for the way he treated people.

It was a period drama about a British aristocrat named Lady Barbara Skelton, who was played by the American actress Faye Dunaway. Lady Skelton marries a rich nobleman but gets bored and, for excitement, turns to robbery and falls for a man she meets on the highway.

It meant going into a lot of period houses and dressing lavish bedrooms and other rooms, and as I was on the dressing crew and with a few of my own mates, it was a real fun time.

The Prop Master was an old friend of mine as well called Eddie Francis, who was a nice man, but as nutty as a bag of frogs, very nervous and was always to be seen with a cigarette in his mouth.

Dealing with Michael Winner was a handful, as he was an absolute control freak and literally trusted no one to do anything. He directed the film, controlled the money flow, and in the end, even edited the film under the pseudonym of Arnold Crust. To say he was tight with the purse strings would have been an understatement.

He even had a young boy at his side carrying his clipboard and megaphone, which he loved to use, and maligned him continually if he slipped up. I couldn't see why the lad put up with this, but he told me he just turned off, took the flack, knowing it was his way into Production, and he's probably a top producer these days. So, as you can see, Michael's way was fear. Not many people stood up to him; he wielded such power and would hire and fire crew on a whim if he felt the need.

The unit had got behind in shooting, so Eddie had asked me to stay on a bit longer, and I found myself dressing Lady Skelton's bedroom located in a period property called 'North Mymms House' in Hertfordshire. Nothing unusual, but this scene called for the sheets on the bed to be black satin.

As we unpacked the crates to dress the bed, there were no black satin sheets to be seen, so I mentioned it to the other Prop, Johnny Palmer. As I had done a lot of standing by, I got in the habit of remembering these sorts of details, as they invariably turned out to be important. You can take the boy out of standing by, but you can't take the standing by out of the boy, so to speak.

John and I checked all the other crates, but it was pretty clear we didn't have them, so John shot off to talk to the Art Department. It was the proverbial hornets' nest, and within minutes they were ransacking the crates just as we had done. The unit and Michael were due in the next half an hour, and no one wanted to start the day with a rollicking from Michael. With his reputation, you might not finish the day.

In 1982, mobile phones were virtually non-existent, so getting hold of the buyer who should have ordered these was no easy task. The Art Director frantically sat on the house phone, calling likely places the buyer might be, to find out what had happened. Finally, he located her. She had thought it was just 'script' talk and had sent some nicer ones with a lace edge. The colour in the Art Director's face visibly drained.

Some choice words were exchanged, and the sheets were ordered to be fast-tracked down to the set, but the problem was it was now 8.10am, and MW would be there in twenty minutes if not before, and no matter how fast a car you had, you would never get from London to North Mymms in twenty minutes.

As a 'visitor' to this film and with nothing to lose, I started to find this really funny. I had never seen so many headless chickens in one place. He really must be the tyrant everyone said he was if he instilled this sort of fear in people when he wasn't even there.

I was told to dress the bed anyway with the nice lace-edged sheets, so we had something to show him and had nearly finished when the great man appeared in the room behind me. There was only me there at the time, and as I turned to acknowledge him, he was very polite and wished me Good Morning, which took me back a bit, all things considered.

"Do you know why the sheets are cream with a laced edge?" he asked as he clocked the bed.

"Not really. Just what I was given," I lied.

"They are supposed to be black satin, as it says in the script," he started.

Now there's the real Michael Winner, I thought.

"I'll get the Art Director, shall I?" I said to him.

The First, Ron Purdie, had arrived and immediately got a few harsh words from MW about the delay to shooting. Ron called for the Art Department so he could pass the buck, and Michael was beginning to shout for everyone under the sun. Why he needed the megaphone when he could shout like this, I don't know.

Sheepishly, the Art Director walked in. He knew what was coming and took both barrels.

"Where are the f**king black satin sheets?" Michael stormed.

"They're on their way," replied the AD as if that would pacify the situation.

"On their way? They should be here on the bed," bellowed MW.

"They're in a fast car as we speak," said the AD trying to pretend everything was under control.

Then Michael delivered the line.

"Fast car. They should be in a f**king helicopter. Don't you ever keep me waiting again."

Vintage Michael!

Anyone involved with this farce was being lambasted by someone or other. Eddie wandered into the middle of it all with the usual cigarette in mouth and twitching like mad, trying to look as if he was doing something to help. He wasn't.

I had wandered off outside looking for the car, and finally it arrived with a very agitated driver looking for help, He was most relieved to get rid of his cargo, and as I walked towards the set with the crate, the AD wrenched it from my grip and raced into the set, trying to retrieve some dignity.

The bed was dressed in record time, and finally Michael could start shooting, but he wasn't finished yet.

"Finally!" he said. "You've cost me an hour of shooting. We'll talk about this later. Now get off my f**king set and let me get on."

I felt for the little lad. He was bound to get the fallout from this, but with his attitude, he probably just closed his eyes, bit his tongue and thought of his career.

To my knowledge, Michael did simmer down, and the Art Department survived a possible coup, but in my eyes, Michael certainly lived up to his reputation.

In later years, when Michael did a commercial in England, he delivered a line that has been mimicked ever since.

With a hysterical lady in the ad, he says, "Calm down dear, it's only a commercial." It always reminds me of that day at North Mymms House when he blew a gasket. Can you imagine his reaction if someone had said to him, "Calm down, Michael, it's only some black sheets?" Their head would have been on a spike at the front gate.

I have met quite a few Directors in my time, all with their own ways of getting the best out of everyone, but I know which way I prefer. It certainly is not the Winner Way.

He went on to make a string of very successful films, so I can only assume from that, there is not just one method of making a film.

It was an awfully long time before I stepped on a feature film set again. My life was changing in so many ways, and so many things had happened that the thought that I would ever be on another film in my lifetime never occurred to me.

Ann and I had done a lot of work on the house, and All-props had finally taken off, giving us another source of finance. George was beginning to come in a lot more, and we had grown so much we had to put a mezzanine floor in and taken over the unit next door. Harry was born in 1989, so our family was growing; Ellie and Ria had settled into their school and were really doing well, and Ann had built up a nice group of friends she socialised with, so our lives were looking very rosy indeed.

On 16th September 1992, all of that changed, literally overnight. The British Government, in its efforts to support the pound, had pushed billions of pounds in, only to see their policy fail. In this country, it was called 'Black Wednesday', and the economic consequences of that day shook us all. Interest rates, for example, shot through the roof, and our mortgage went from 5.6% to 15.6% virtually within days. Businesses crashed, house prices slumped, leaving many people in negative equity on their houses. Unemployment rose dramatically, and the country just fell apart.

The film industry, including commercials, took a nosedive, and hardly anything was being made. The repercussions of this on our lives were enormous, and with so little work around, my earnings plummeted, and with no productions, there was no one hiring props, so Allprops income dropped at a time when we had just invested large sums for new floors and a second unit.

Everyone was so badly hit. Their cosy lifestyles were no longer cosy, and a friend of ours who used to buy and sell houses took it so hard that the financial strains pushed him over the edge, and he killed himself, leaving a wife and two young children. It was a horrendous time for all, and we weren't exempt.

With hardly any income and our mortgage running at nearly £2000 per month, and with the girls at private school, I seriously didn't know myself how we were going to survive this. I had to find money from somewhere just to get through each week and delved into so many different projects there was barely enough time in the day to do anything else but work and sleep. This put a huge strain on our marriage, like everyone else's, and I think, sadly, it was the beginning of the end of our marriage.

On the work front, the Producers took full advantage of the situation, started throwing out many of the work practices the Union had demanded, and put in rules more favourable to them. They totally had the upper hand at this time, and it never went back to power days for the Unions. You either worked the way the producer wanted you to, or you didn't work at all, and a proposed strike by the crew to protest against these changes fizzled out to nothing when crew desperate to pay their bills just didn't turn up on the strike days, but took any work that was offered.

It took years for things to settle down and people to start rebuilding their lives, but somehow, and I don't really know how we did it, we survived, kept our house and managed to keep Allprops afloat, where many businesses never recovered.

As the years went by, work picked up, and so did Allprops, and it was one day when I was there that Les phoned me about a film he had started as Prop Master, based at Twickenham, called 'Little Voice'. It starred Jane Horrocks and Michael Caine, and he wanted me to help him out for a few weeks dressing some sets.

It wasn't difficult for me to get away these days as Allprops had grown so much, and we had employed some really good, competent staff, who you could happily leave to run the place in the short term.

After the slump in 1992, the film industry was booming again, and he was finding it difficult to get men, so I reluctantly agreed to help him as he had helped me so many times in the past.

I had gotten out of the swing of things being a Prop Man, particularly on films, as I hadn't done a full film in nearly 12 years. It was strange being back, but the sight of seeing some of the old faces again soon put me at my ease, and I threw myself into it.

This was the 21st feature film I had worked on, and it was definitely going to be my last as just being back made me realise that I didn't want to do this any more and Allprops is where I should be. I began to resent being there, but I had promised Les, so stuck it out.

It is strange how life can go sometimes. I knew this would be my last film, and in a few days it would all be over.

Then, one day after dressing a set where Michael Caine does his drunken version of Frank Sinatra's 'I did it My Way', where his whole world is falling apart around him, and he transposes the words to 'I did it my f**king way', Michael came on set to do his bit.

It was such a classic moment I had to stay and watch it, and I am so glad that I did. He had finished and was leaving the set. I was standing with a cup of tea as he walked past and then stopped and turned back to me.

"We've worked together, haven't we?" he said.

I was so taken aback.

"On 'Water'," I replied.

"That's right. Thought I knew your face. How are you?"

"Good, thanks." I didn't really know what to say.

"Nice seeing you again," he said and wandered off.

I stood there momentarily, wondering if that had just happened. One of the biggest names in films had just remembered me after not seeing each other for over 13 years. Now, how nice was that? He really was such a genuine person, and the thought that he had acknowledged me when he could have easily walked straight past was a great memory to have; and on my last film. It seemed fitting somehow.

"And not many people know that!"

CHAPTER 29

FINAL THOUGHTS

Towards the end of the century, there were big changes happening in my life.

Ann and I were sadly not getting on well. I think our ideas of life had gone in different directions, and our differences were never going to be reconciled. We had tried to ignore this to a certain extent and carry on as the kids were still young, Harry in particular, but the plain truth was our marriage was over. Ann had a little circle of good friends she liked to spend her time with, and as much as I didn't like the amount of time she wasn't there, it didn't bother me as much as it should have done. I suppose it made up for the times I wasn't there due to work.

Making the actual decision to split took a while. For me, it was the hardest one I've had to make in my life, but it had to be made as living in the same house because of the children, where everyone was miserable for one reason or other due to the situation, we all knew existed, became unbearable.

I didn't feel married any more, and I'm sure Ann felt the same, so after some very sad conversations, we decided to call it a day. Everyone was upset, as you can imagine, and the fear of what would happen next was prominent in all our minds, but in the end, it would be the right thing to do.

Our forever house would have to be sold, and Ann and I would have to get our own separate places. Fortunately, with the improvements we had made and general house price increases in the area, we came out with enough money, after paying the mortgage off, to be able to do that and found smaller houses quite close to each other, so seeing the kids would not be a problem or too much disruption for them.

The odd thing about all of this was that we had bought from a couple who were getting a divorce, and we were selling because of our divorce. The couple who did buy our house subsequently sold it some years later, as they were getting divorced as well. Spooky, eh?

For those of you that have unfortunately had to go through a divorce, you have my deepest sympathies. It was horrible, although necessary, and I felt so much sadness when I saw how Ellie, Ria and Harry were affected by all of this. As much as you wanted to be able to fix all their hurt, there wasn't much you could do but let time do its healing, which, thank God, seems to have happened.

Ann went on to have new relationships, and I, myself, met a lovely lady called Clare who had her own daughter, Kimberley, and in the year 2000, we got married and have been together ever since.

Clare and I met on a commercial as she was helping out in the Art Department, strangely with Belinda, who had first got me into commercials. Now there's odd.

We did a bit of work with each other before I persuaded her to give up her side of things and come and work with me at Allprops, where I was now full time.

She was reluctant at first, but after a crash course in the accounts department, which Sally, George's wife, had been running, she took over when Sally decided to give up working in there and threw Clare in at the deep end.

She did well and reinvented our systems, transforming our cash flow, which gave us so much so more manoeuvrability. We expanded a lot, built another floor in the second unit and made Allprops a name that everyone in the industry knew. Over the years, my other partners sold off their shares and Clare and I became the sole directors until we were finally bought out by a bigger company in 2007.

Allprops had been around for over 20 years, and we had employed a load of really nice people. Ellie, Ria, and Harry worked there at some time, and even Ann worked there for a while, along with numerous other great individuals. My mum came in and helped once when we were busy; God bless her.

I have to say a special mention, though, to one person who came to work for us as a boy and left a man, as they say. Joe Green.

I remember we needed to employ an extra person, and Joe had turned up for an interview, lacking in confidence and probably not expecting to get the job. He gave me his CV, and I gave it back, to his surprise. I personally think CVs aren't worth the paper they are written on, merely full of boastful statements to make you seem better. I preferred to see what the person was like themselves, and he came over really well, so he got the job.

He never let us down and transformed himself from the timid lad that turned up for the interview into an outgoing, confident individual that started making and acting in his own films, took part in period re-enactments of battles and became a real asset to Allprops, staying with us to the bitter end, when many had long departed. We are still in touch to this day, and we count him as one of our dear friends.

Whenever we talk, he reminisces about the good old days and how he has never found a job that equalled it. Now that is nice to hear.

He was right, though, Allprops was a great place to work,

and we had a lot of laughs, and a lot of funny things happened there which would also make a nice book, such as being raided by the bomb squad when a dummy bomb we had hired out was sent by this demented idiot to the Prime Minister, and after being detected was safely exploded, but our hire label on it remained intact. And there's more where that came from.

My life could have taken a much different path to the one that eventually came my way. I was literally floundering down in Folkestone, not knowing what to do to make things better for my family, until an unexpected visit from Les changed all that. That sliding doors moment, where if I hadn't made the decision to try what he suggested, would have resulted in who knows what.

I don't think it would have given me everything that the film industry did, taking me to parts of the world I probably wouldn't have visited, meeting people I might have only seen at the cinemas, staying in great hotels and earning more than I ever expected which gave my kids the best start in life that I could possibly give them.

I would never have met all the great people I worked with and made lifelong friends with, the likes of Denis and George and many others, and if I hadn't met Denis, then Allprops may never have been conceived. All those who passed through Allprops would have had their lives changed as well. The mind boggles at the delicate nature of life and its passages that can alter in the blink of an eye with a decision you do or don't make.

Back in 1978, I certainly made the right decision.

Writing this book has been a real pleasure, and it has revived a load of memories that had sat at the back of my mind for so long I'd forgotten they existed. It has also laid down a record for my children of what was happening to me and what I was doing all those times I couldn't be with them. It was a difficult decision to make, one which I am sure many parents have wrestled with, as to whether doing a job you don't particularly like so you can spend more time at home and have fewer resources to be able to provide for your family is better than being away and earning more so you can improve their futures, in a job you enjoy doing.

Decisions are what you have to make in life, and however they turn out, you have to stand by them as you generally make them based on the information you have available at the time. Hindsight is a wonderful thing but no good to you when you have to make your mind up and act.

Yes, I often wondered if I had made correct judgements as I went through my life. We could have stayed in Folkestone. Maybe Ann and I would still be together if we had; who knows? I fear not.

Decisions were made, and I like to think they were the right ones for us all. I have had a very fortunate career and look back on it with fond regard. There were many laughs and great experiences, and if I am honest, in a very selfish way, it suited me down to the ground. I collected a lot of photos from the films I worked on and hoped to include some of them in this book, but after 40 years, getting copyright clearance was proving to be a nightmare, so they stay in my album as a lasting memory.

All I know is that I wouldn't have been able to have done any of this without the support of all my family and friends, and to all of them, past and present, I dedicate this book and hope they enjoy reading it, and if they like it, tell someone else about it.

To my brother, Les, my mum, Mary and my dad, Charlie, I wish you were still here to read this. I miss you all so very much.

THE END

ABOUT ATMOSPHERE PRESS

Atmosphere Press is an independent, full-service publisher for excellent books in all genres and for all audiences. Learn more about what we do at atmospherepress.com.

We encourage you to check out some of Atmosphere's latest releases, which are available at Amazon.com and via order from your local bookstore:

Finding Us, by Kristin Rehkamp

The Ideological and Political System of Banselism, by Royard Halmonet Vantion (Ancheng Wang)

Unconditional: Loving and Losing an Addict, by Lizzy and Adam

Telling Tales and Sharing Secrets, by Jackie Collins, Diana Kinared, and Sally Showalter

Nursing Homes: A Missionary's Journey Through Heaven's Waiting Room, by Tim Eatman Ph.D.

Timeline of Stars, by Joe Adcock

A Boy Who Loved Me, by Wilson Semitti

The Injustice in Justice, by Charmaine Loverin

Living in the Gray, by Katie Weber

Living with Veracity, Dying with Dignity, by Alison Clay-Duboff

Noah's Rejects, by Rob Kagan

A lot of Questions (with no answers)?, by Jordan Neben

Cowboy from Prague: An Immigrant's Pursuit of the American Dream, by Charles Ota Heller

Sleeping Under the Bridge, by Melissa Baker

The Only Prayer I Ever Have to Say Is Thank You, by M. Kaya Hill

Amygdala Blue, by Paul Lomax

A Caregiver's Love Story, by Nancie Wiseman Attwater

ABOUT THE AUTHOR

PETER BENSON was born in London in 1950. After obtaining a BA in Business Finance he pursued a career in business. It was not for him, so in 1978 he became a film Prop Man.

He worked on some of the biggest British made films over the course of 25 years, during which time he started a successful Prop Hire company in 1984, before retiring in 2007.

He now lives in Kent, England, with his wife Clare and her daughter, Kimberley, closer to his grown-up children Ellenna, Ria and Harry.

Printed in Great Britain
by Amazon

22905081R00108